Flywheel

Transformational Leadership Coaching for Sustainable Change

Elle Allison-Napolitano

Foreword by Rob and Kathy Bocchino

CORWIN
A SAGE Company

FOR INFORMATION:

Corwin

A SAGE Company

2455 Teller Road

Thousand Oaks, California 91320

(800) 233-9936

www.corwin.com

SAGE Publications Ltd.

1 Oliver's Yard

55 City Road

London EC1Y 1SP

United Kingdom

SAGE Publications India Pvt. Ltd.

B 1/I 1 Mohan Cooperative Industrial Area

Mathura Road, New Delhi 110 044

India

SAGE Publications Asia-Pacific Pte. Ltd.

3 Church Street

#10-04 Samsung Hub

Singapore 049483

Acquisitions Editor: Arnis Burvikovs

Associate Editor: Desirée A. Bartlett

Editorial Assistants: Mayan White and Ariel Price

Production Editor: Melanie Birdsall

Copy Editor: Janet Ford

Typesetter: C&M Digitals (P) Ltd.

Proofreader: Victoria Reed-Castro

Indexer: Molly Hall

Cover Designer: Rose Storey

Permissions Editor: Jennifer Barron

Printed in the United States of America.

Library of Congress Cataloging-in-Publication Data

Allison-Napolitano, Elle.

Flywheel : transformational leadership coaching for sustainable change / Elle Allison-Napolitano.

pages cm

Includes bibliographical references and index.

ISBN 978-1-4522-6091-4 (pbk.)

1. Executive coaching. 2. Leadership—Study and teaching. I. Title.

HD30.4.A455 2013

658.4'07124—dc23   2013014806

This book is printed on acid-free paper.

13 14 15 16 17 10 9 8 7 6 5 4 3 2 1

Contents

PART II. PROJECTS

Tools and additional materials related to *Flywheel*
can be accessed at **www.WisdomOut.com**
and at **www.Corwin.com/Flywheel.**

Foreword

Most likely you are holding this book because you are searching for something. That's probably a good sign: real leaders are almost always looking further down the road, beyond what they can currently see. Maybe the thing you are seeking is some wisdom that is just beyond your grasp or maybe it is some truth that you have lost along the way. Perhaps you see that others around you (or who report to you) have great, yet unfulfilled potential. Perhaps you are looking for ways to open the organization so the best ideas and opportunities are heard and realized instead of lost. Whatever it is, Elle Allison-Napolitano understands the journey and from her research and experience she points the way to the path with heart. For Elle, and for you, leadership means finding practical, field-tested ways to empower, to develop, and to support others.

Flywheel is the pathway for leaders to learn how to coach others to achieve what they could not, or would not do on their own. At its heart, this is a book about the kinds of skilled conversations and interactions that leaders can have that engage, develop, and empower; it is about how leaders can be transformational coaches.

The title of the book comes from a simple idea of what a flywheel does. In a watch, the flywheel stores and balances energy. In systems, balancing energy is one of the key functions of leadership. But how? *Flywheel* provides a constellation of practical skills, steps, and protocols for leaders to support other leaders through coaching, both formally and informally. Through examples, stories, and research, Elle Allison-Napolitano provides a set of coaching skills that are nothing short of transformational. Here you will learn how to go beyond putting out fires and managing the status quo. Leaders who embrace this practice find ways to be more conscious and present and they are more ready to help others face and meet the challenging realities of the 21st century.

To do this successfully and ecologically requires a frame of mind that is open to the kinds of game-changing initiatives that make a real and meaningful difference. Transformational coaching unearths and challenges limiting assumptions, as by definition, it must. It also means leaders must have specific, hands-on skills and protocols right from the start. In *Flywheel* you will learn about when, where, and how to listen well, and why this is such a demanding essential leadership skill. In addition, you will learn how to deepen and assure understanding, and the power and skills of asking real questions that foster thinking, learning, and problem-solving.

Leaders step forward to start, revitalize, and champion organizational initiatives for positive change. In the Flywheel model, this means having real, concrete projects with deadlines, deliverables, and real-life effects. It also means leaders need practical protocols like the eight steps of the Powerful Coaching Conversation, and ways to initiate a coaching contract. It means developing and helping others develop the passion for doing "the greater good" instead of "business as usual." This work provides templates, diagnostic charts, protocols, and other tools to facilitate these kinds of important coaching conversations.

We have known Elle Allison-Napolitano for more than 20 years; we first met her in her role as supervisor of school improvement. She has always been an advocate for the kinds of developmental interventions outlined and explained in this book. Her life journey has followed this path with depth, authenticity, and integrity. Her work has taken her all over the planet and has been dedicated to this, whether it has been in her role as school leader, as coach, or as an international consultant. All of these endeavors, and her work at Wisdom Out reflect not only practical hard-won lessons that she is willing to so generously share, but also her delightful, brilliant, and engaging personality. Elle is an engaging story-teller, an amazing teacher, and a wonderful person. You will get to know and learn from her in this book, and you will be better for it. And it will take work.

We recommend this work wholeheartedly and without reservation of any kind.

—*Rob and Kathy Bocchino*
Heart of Change Associates
Carolina Beach, North Carolina, 2013

Preface

Following a conference where I led a breakout session on the topic of leadership coaching, a superintendent from the audience who was particularly enthused about the exercises on listening I conducted with the group, took me aside to share a personal story. "Joe" told me he was lucky to work in his district with so many people who were true leaders in every sense of the word. However, as Joe tells the story, this wasn't always the case, and he takes most of the blame for it. He said, "I knew I was working with administrators and teachers who were smart, well-educated, and experienced. And yet, they were always incredibly busy and overwhelmed. They were good at putting out fires, but they did not build the future." One day, Joe went to work with a bad case of laryngitis. He literally could not talk, he could only listen. He made a sign for his door that said, *"I have laryngitis and I can't talk. You can still meet with me, but all I can do is listen—sorry."*

When a few of his colleagues stopped by and joked with Joe about how good it felt to talk when he could not do anything but listen, he smiled and nodded. But, by the time the tenth person came by and made the same joke, it suddenly dawned on him: he was a poor listener. As the day went on, something else became clear to Joe. The people he worked with were full of good ideas, creativity, and passion for their work and for education. It's just that he never listened long enough for them to get that far in the conversation. That day, Joe made a commitment to learn how to listen, and that led him to discover what it meant to be a leader who is also a coach. "I have to wonder," Joe told me with a shake of his head, "what did I prevent people from contributing, before I saw myself as a coaching leader?"

WHY FLYWHEEL, WHY NOW

Admittedly, I am a coaching geek. I love all things coaching and I never cease to be fascinated and downright thrilled by the effect coaching has on leaders who are determined to make a big difference in their organizations. In education, this translates to benefits for students—and who wouldn't be impressed by leadership that empowers young folks to make good lives for themselves?

I invented Flywheel so that leaders can make big moves in education and in their lives. Interestingly enough, big moves that make a difference in education require incredible and sustained focus, without which deep implementation is never achieved. Mike Schmoker makes this point early in his book titled *Focus* (2011). Schmoker says that if educators really want to improve schools, they need to focus on well-known approaches, specifically, "a common curriculum, sound lessons, and authentic literacy" (p. 9). Schmoker's point is that educators already know what works. As he sees it, the problem is that "we have never fully clarified them or obsessed over their implementation." Leadership coaching is a personalized strategy for just that—for mobilizing the energy of leaders to obsess on deep implementation of what works and for taking action to make systemic and sustainable change.

Flywheel?

It was a high school physics teacher in one of my workshops a few years ago who made the observation that leadership coaching was a "flywheel" to the hard work of leaders. Flywheel? This teacher, who was at the helm of his school's transformation to a science magnet center explained to me that a flywheel is a mechanical invention that stores energy, which can be called on and used to keep things moving when the energy source is no longer available. Aha! I know about flywheels from those grueling spin classes I take at the gym. If you've ever been in a spin class, most likely the stationary bike you rode utilized a large single flywheel that you could adjust to simulate the demands of the open road, from a nice flat course (where the flywheel is transferring a lot of energy to the pedals) to a steep hill (where less energy is transferred to the pedals). For the physics teacher in my coaching class, coaching conversations created energy for him— energy for sustaining the obsessive focus that Mike Schmoker writes about.

WHAT MAKES FLYWHEEL DIFFERENT FROM OTHER LEADERSHIP COACHING APPROACHES

Leadership coaching is not a new idea. Every professional field, including education, cares about developing leaders who are capable of managing complex systems. But, while traditional leadership coaching programs focus on increasing personal and organizational performance (Storber & Grant, 2006), Flywheel is an approach to leadership coaching that expands the expectations of leadership from managing the inevitable challenges of day-to-day operations, to developing leaders capable of changing the organization for the better. Grounded in ideas from transformation theory, Flywheel is geared for leaders who are at the helm of important work, especially when they begin important projects or take current initiatives to deeper levels of implementation.

> Flywheel is an approach to leadership coaching that expands the expectations of leaders from managing the inevitable challenges of day-to-day operations, to developing leaders capable of changing the organization for the better.

A Transformational Approach

In his book *Education Unbound*, Frederick Hess (2010) candidly writes, "The biggest challenge we face is not a lack of potential practices or good ideas, but systemic rigidity that makes it difficult to execute even smart solutions with discipline and focus" (p. 130). Hess's observation draws to mind Einstein's famous quote, "You cannot solve a problem from the same consciousness that created it. You must learn to see the world anew." Thus, Flywheel embraces a transformational approach to change. This means that it employs tools and processes that pierce the limiting assumptions that prevent people and systems from discovering breakthroughs and solving the most vexing problems in education. It provides a way for leaders to *do* meaningful work while simultaneously *becoming* leaders

WHAT MAKES FLYWHEEL DIFFERENT FROM OTHER LEADERSHIP COACHING MODELS

1. It develops leadership for change, not just managing day-to-day challenges.
2. It's geared especially for leaders at the helm of crucial projects in the organization.
3. It's designed for any leader at any level in the system, not limited to administrators.
4. It seeks to rewire the system for sustainable change—not just implement good ideas that never take hold.
5. It helps leaders deepen their leadership abilities through focus on real work and real issues in the organization.

who do meaningful work and who rewire the organization to support and sustain new ways to assure that schools work for all students.

Flywheel is also different from many other leadership coaching models in that it is not limited to leaders in formal administrative positions in the hierarchy of the organization. Instead, Flywheel invites leaders at all levels in the system to step up to the helm of important work that actually shapes the future. Regardless of their position in the organization—principals, teacher leaders, administrators (you name it)—Flywheel supports people who see themselves or come to see themselves as activists, innovators, deep implementers, leaders, and change agents.

THE STRUCTURE OF THIS BOOK

This book is divided into four main parts:

Part I is called *Promise*, which includes two chapters that describe what a transformational approach to leadership coaching can produce for individuals, leaders, and organizations. The first chapter in *Promise* lays out the concepts of transformation theory and relates them to leadership and to the process of leadership coaching. In this chapter, the story of Carrie and Sarah, two leaders engaged in leadership coaching helps you see transformation theory in action. The second chapter in *Promise* focuses on the benefits that come when all leaders see themselves as coaches. These benefits include job-embedded professional development, developing leadership capacity, and leveraging and sustaining their own energy for important work.

Part II of this book is called *Projects*, and describes the transformational change work most worthy of leadership coaching. Chapter 3 explores how leadership coaches assist leaders in identifying projects that have the potential to change education for a greater good. Chapter 4 provides ideas and tools for leadership coaches to use to inspire leaders to take action and get important work moving in the first 100 days.

Part III of this book is titled *Practice*. Part III contains the most number of chapters (Chapters 5, 6, 7, 8, and 9), each one focused on the actual process of leadership coaching. My hope is that after you read the chapters in Part III, you begin to use all or some of the ideas to coach your colleagues and peers.

- Chapter 5 is an overview of the Flywheel system. It describes all of the elements to use if you provide long-term coaching to colleagues and peers.
- Chapter 6 takes one of the elements in the system, the Powerful Coaching Conversation, and provides an overview of all eight of the steps in the conversation protocol. In this chapter, there is also a pacing chart that helps you plan out coaching sessions that last anywhere from 30 minutes to 75 minutes.
- Chapters 7 through 10 focus on crucial coaching communication skills.
  - Chapter 7 is called *Listen, Just Listen* and as you might expect, it focuses entirely on the critical coaching communication skill of listening.
  - Chapter 8 is called *Question Assumptions and Deepen Understanding*, and teaches you how to use summaries, paraphrases, and to ask clarifying and detail questions in order to help the leaders you coach uncover assumptions and make potentially transformational discoveries. In this chapter you also learn how to use the mental model known as The Ladder of Inference, as a parallel tool for asking questions.

o Chapter 9 is called *Thought Leadership Questions* and teaches you to ask questions that put ideas on the table designed to inspire insight and innovation in your coachees.

o Chapter 10 is called *The Jaunty Walk*. This chapter pulls together the final stages of the Powerful Coaching Conversation that lead your coachees to make strong commitments to take action, which over time accumulate to the point where real change is visible.

Part IV, *Progress,* contains two chapters and is the final section in this book. Chapter 11 describes considerations and approaches for measuring the impact of leadership coaching. Chapter 12 ends this book with encouragement for making leadership coaching a movement in your organization. It contains myriad strategies that ultimately create a pervasive culture of leadership coaching; a culture where leaders embrace coaching for themselves and for others.

BENEFITS FOR INDIVIDUALS AND ORGANIZATIONS

The main message of this book is that transformational leadership coaching is an essential strategy for supporting and sustaining educational leaders who are engaged in meaningful work in order to achieve results that change the organization for the better. The benefits from applying the ideas presented in this book are many:

- More people interacting with each other through coaching—an approach that empowers and builds efficacy in others.
- More leaders emerging from within the system to assume positions of leadership.
- More people feeling confident about tackling challenging but important projects to advance the goals of the organization.
- An engaged workforce: employees fully participating in the most important initiatives of the organization.
- Ownership and accountability for important work.
- Increased happiness in the workforce through improved relationships, conversations, and interactions on the job.
- More people interacting with each other in ways that spur innovation.
- More people accomplishing meaningful work.
- Wise and timely decisions and solutions to challenges, quandaries, and problems.
- A renewed workforce with energy to achieve even more meaningful work.

WHO THIS BOOK IS FOR

This book is for anyone who wants to know how to use a transformational approach to leadership coaching in order to engage, influence, and support their peers and colleagues as they accomplish meaningful work. In education, leaders who want to add coaching to their leadership repertoire come from the site level, district level, state level, and university level. These savvy leaders understand that their primary job is to develop the leadership capacity of the people they work with and/or supervise, and they want to learn how to coach others on the job, and on the fly.

Specifically, these groups of leaders will find value in reading *Flywheel*:

1. Administrators and teacher leaders who want to add coaching as a leadership strategy for supporting and sustaining colleagues, peers, and direct reports. These individuals are principals, assistant principals, deans, department chairs, teacher leaders of professional learning communities, superintendents, assistant superintendents, regional directors, program supervisors, and curriculum coordinators.

2. Individuals who identify themselves as coaches and for whom coaching is one of their primary responsibilities. These coaches may work internal or external to the school/district/university/organization or they may work for an agency that provides leadership coaching to leaders in these systems.

3. Supervisors/directors/mentors of coaching programs who make decisions about the professional development they wish to provide for the coaches they supervise.

4. Senior leaders who want to create a culture of coaching to build leadership capacity throughout the organization, and who want the administrators they employ to adopt a coaching approach in their management/leadership style as they work with the people they supervise.

5. Leaders who want to know what to expect from a leadership coach, should they choose to work with one.

> Download tools and access other resources at www.WisdomOut.com and at www.Corwin.com/Flywheel.

OPPORTUNITIES FOR CONTINUED LEARNING

In addition to the many tools found between the covers of this book, I also invite you to come to www.Corwin.com/Flywheel and to www.WisdomOut.com to download them for handy and convenient use. When you visit the Wisdom Out website, you also have the chance to register for complimentary webinars on leadership and leadership coaching that further illuminate the ideas presented in this book.

Acknowledgments

First, my gratitude goes to the many educators who have attended my workshops to learn the skills of leadership coaching, and to the leaders who allow me to serve as their leadership coach. The narratives in this book are really their stories; this book is just a conduit for their wisdom.

I also wish to acknowledge a number of individuals whose influence on me is seen on the pages of this book: Michael Fullan, Mike Schmoker, Peter Senge, Paul Axtell, Frederick Hess, Ron Richards, Jody Leinenwever, Tracee Grigsby-Turner, Sue Page, Maggie Cuellar, Janine Hoke, Doreen Corrente, Debbie Lee, Rob and Kathy Bocchino, Bette Frasier, and Len Dose.

I owe the reality of this book to the kind judgment of Arnis Burvikovs and Desirée Bartlett from Corwin. Arnis first gave me the green light to write it when he contacted me to ask if I would write a different book. He and Desirée gave their hearty support to me as I produced both. Also from Corwin, I am grateful to the coordination, editing, and production work of Mayan White, Ariel Price, Melanie Birdsall, Kim Greenberg, Lauren Schroeder, and Janet Ford.

Finally, I thank my smart and handsome husband Len who *always* supports me and never complains about my writing schedule. He pays attention to my ideas, asks me great questions, makes me laugh, removes obstacles, keeps everything running in the house, takes me on surprise dates, amuses the dog, and cooks pasta for us every single Friday night.

PUBLISHER'S ACKNOWLEDGMENTS

Corwin gratefully acknowledges the contributions of the following reviewers:

Dr. Ann W. Davis
Clinical Assistant Professor
The University of North Carolina at Greensboro
Greensboro, NC

Jason Ellingson
Superintendent
Collins-Maxwell CSD
Maxwell, IA

Laura Flynn
Instructional Coach
Los Ranchos Elementary School
Albuquerque, NM

Dr. Tracee Grigsby-Turner
Supervisor of Professional Development
Alief ISD
Houston, TX

About the Author

 **Elle Allison-Napolitano,** Founder of Wisdom Out, specializes in leadership development and organizational learning. Dr. Allison-Napolitano works with leaders, aspiring leaders, senior leadership teams, school teams, and leadership coaches to teach them the strategies, practices, and tools they need to increase their organization's capacity for sustainable change.

Elle has been a teacher, principal, supervisor of school improvement, assistant superintendent, educational consultant, and leadership coach. She earned her PhD in Organizational Learning from the University of New Mexico. She is a graduate of the National Staff Development's Council's Academy and is a member of the National Speakers Association. She is author of several books and articles on leadership renewal and resilience and on leadership coaching.

Elle lives in the San Francisco Bay area with her husband Len and their 16-year-old Vizsla dog named "Olé." Contact Elle at elle@wisdomout.com for customized workshops, leadership academies, boot camps, and keynotes. To register for the Wisdom Out newsletter and monthly complimentary webinars, please visit www.WisdomOut.com.

Part I

Promise

The Meaning of Transformational Leadership Coaching  chapter 1

Structures of which we are unaware hold us prisoner.

—Peter Senge *(The Fifth Discipline: The Art and Practice of the Learning Organization, 1990, p. 94)*

Although Flywheel draws on many different theories, all of them cogent to organizational and leadership change, transformation theory is fundamental to the Flywheel approach. This chapter provides readers with a foundational understanding of transformation theory as it applies to leadership coaching. The story of Carrie and Sarah provides us with an example.

A STORY OF TRANSFORMATIONAL LEADERSHIP

Carrie and Sarah, two regional superintendents from a large urban school district in the south (the names have been changed, but the story is true) participate together in leadership coaching and use it to focus on their most passionate work: developing principal leadership capacity throughout the district.

As you might expect, Carrie and Sarah are troubled when school leadership teams do not click; when the principals, team leaders, deans, and others either cannot or will not leverage their leadership skills to create powerful and collaborative teams capable of leading students' learning. When dysfunctional teams exist then everyone, including Carrie and Sarah, must divert their energy away from the priorities of meaningful work.

Inspired by their new superintendent's commitment to building leadership capacity, and fueled by a deep and unwavering devotion to the schools they supervise, Carrie and Sarah made it their shared project to examine the current approach to leadership selection and development in the district. They were determined to devote their leadership coaching sessions on taking action to move this project forward.

Over time, Carrie and Sarah's coaching conversations shifted from initially focusing on interventions when leadership teams fail, such as moving individuals to different schools, which often created a cascade of logistical personnel problems in the organization, to eventually focusing on engendering a craving for leadership team success right from the start, for each new, novice, and aspiring administrator. As their leadership coach, I recall the change in their language that signaled this paradigm shift. Instead of talking about *leadership growth plans* (which describe interventions *after* relationships and effectiveness have soured), Carrie and Sarah began describing what they ultimately decided to call *leadership success plans* (plans for success right from the start, beginning with recruitment and the interview process).

Transformation Theory

Put forth by Jack Mezirow in 1978, transformation theory identifies the processes by which adults come to question their assumptions and those of others, and arrive at new perspectives. In other words, transformation theory is about change—dramatic change that shapes people and organizations and makes them visibly different to themselves and others (Merriam & Caffarella, 1999).

Adult learning specialists Merriam and Caffarella (1999) tell us that transformation theory involves a change in perspective that " . . . is personally emancipating in that one is freed from previously held beliefs, attitudes, values, and feelings that have constricted and distorted one's life" (p. 320). More than being set free from these binding ideas, transformation theory also holds that the person finally understands *how* they were held hostage by previous beliefs, which allows them to consciously choose differently in new situations. Carrie and Sarah's story beautifully illustrates the experience of transformation.

Catalyzed by feeling ill at ease with the current approach for responding to dysfunctional school leadership teams, Carrie and Sarah's experience is transformational in that they ultimately challenged and freed themselves of assumptions that limited their options. This is seen in their paradigm shift *from* remediation and intervention *to* prevention and empowerment. Unburdened by beliefs that previously stymied them, Carrie and Sarah gained a new perspective, which generated a whole new set of possible actions. These actions are likely to create profound improvement, not just in the ways that leadership teams function once they are in place, but systemically from the recruitment and interview process, to professional development for leaders, to the long-term administrative supervision and evaluation process.

The journey ahead of them will no doubt have its ups and downs (meaningful change never comes easily), but Carrie and Sarah feel a renewed sense of energy toward their aspirational goal of sustaining strong and effective leadership teams in every school.

With Carrie and Sarah's story serving as an example, we can more clearly understand what it means to be a transformational leader and what it means to provide transformational leadership coaching.

Transformation Seen Through Carrie and Sarah's Story

Returning to the story of Carrie and Sarah, we can analyze the assumptions underlying transformation theory as constructed by Mezirow (2000, p. 22), who acknowledges the process does not always follow the phases exactly, but does seem to include some variation of the following:

- **A disorienting dilemma: An awakening, change, loss, or challenge**

  In Carrie and Sarah's story, the disorienting dilemma was the unrest and edginess they felt about the processes in place for responding to dysfunctional leadership teams and the subsequent havoc they produced in the system.

- **Self-examination sometimes accompanied by feelings of self-recrimination, anger, fear, or guilt**

  In one coaching session, Carrie and Sarah sorted through the complex emotions that came with the territory of supervision, including their frustration and disappointment when their interventions did not work. They knew there had to be a better way.

- **A critical assessment of the assumptions underlying one's beliefs and perspectives up until this point**

  Carrie and Sarah made a huge leap in their thinking when they broke through the assumptions that dictated that the only way to create functional leadership teams was if they had full control over forming the teams in the first place, or if they took action once they were aware of problems. Once they released those assumptions, and replaced them with the perspective that leadership success begins with the recruitment and interview process, and that everyone has room for improvement, they saw new possibilities, including a set of strategies for building leadership capacity in others.

- **Recognition that other leaders also experience discontent and processes of transformation**

  Carrie and Sarah accepted the challenges inherent in complex systems. They realize that other leaders grapple with similar issues, and believe that they too will handle whatever comes up.

- **Exploration of options for new roles, relationships, and actions**

  When Carrie and Sarah realized they wanted to establish leadership success plans with each new administrator hired, they set up meetings with each new administrator and the superintendent, during which time they connected the leadership success plan to the administrator evaluation protocol.

- **Planning a new course of action consistent with the new paradigm**

  During this phase, Carrie and Sarah lingered over the pros and cons of leadership growth plans versus leadership success plans.

- **Acquiring knowledge and skills for implementing one's plan, provisional trying of new roles and building competence, and self-confidence in new roles and relationships**

  Before Carrie and Sarah held meetings with each new administrator and the superintendent, they scheduled a work session with each other to comb through the current administrator evaluation instrument in order to locate ambiguous language and clarify each point with examples from the district. Because of this process, Carrie and Sarah became facile with relating the two-dimensional leadership expectations on the evaluation instrument to the three-dimensional expectations of leaders on the job.

- **Reintegration into one's life and work on the basis of conditions congruent with the new perspective**

  Carrie and Sarah began to think that the Leadership Success Plan was a good idea and helpful tool for all of the principals they supervised, not just the new and novice principals. They planned opportunities to communicate to site leadership teams that lifelong learning is part and parcel of leadership excellence, and that the supervision and evaluation process is meant to expand their capacity for leadership. This plan brings them back full circle to serving one of the most strategic goals of their organization: building leadership capacity in all. However, now they approach this work with a transformed perspective that feels empowering and energizing.

As you reflect on the story of Carrie and Sarah through the eyes of a leadership coach, you begin to discern the fundamental beliefs underpinning transformational change. Before you continue reading, use the space provided below to write your predictions about the assumptions underlying transformation theory as it applies to leadership coaching. Then, read the next section and see how your predictions compare.

_____

_____

_____

_____

_____

TRANSFORMATIONAL LEADERSHIP COACHING

Transformational leadership coaching is an organizational strategy for leadership development that is based on the qualities of transformation theory and transformational leadership, and employs processes and tools designed to help leaders remove obstructive assumptions and beliefs that limit their greatness. Once free of these limitations, and empowered by their new vision and story, these leaders catalyze leadership in the people around them and create needed change throughout their organizations in order to produce remarkable results.

The tools and processes you find in this book facilitate transformational leadership development, and display a bias for bold action that leads to profound results

> **BELIEFS EMBRACED BY TRANSFORMATIONAL LEADERSHIP COACHES**
>
> - Leaders come to coaching with wisdom and experience about their work.
> - A person's frame of reference (how they understand the world) is composed of assumptions that selectively shape and restrict expectations.
> - People transform their frame of reference through critical reflection of assumptions.
> - Transformative learning emancipates people from unquestioning acceptance of what they've come to know.
> - Learners need to be at the center of contextual learning—not receivers of information and expert advice.
> - Experience combined with reflective discourse creates learning.

Leadership coaches who approach their work through this lens embrace these beliefs and translate them into practice.

THE TRANSFORMATIONAL LEADER

I do not mean to suggest that transformational leadership coaching is the only way to create leaders who are capable of transformational change. However, leadership coaching grounded in the precepts of transformational change is designed explicitly to promote transformational leadership.

Agents of Change

Transformational leaders are what Michael Fullan calls "change agents" (Fullan, 1993). Change agents are individuals who have a strong moral purpose and have the ability to skillfully engage in the process of change. Change agents, regardless of their formal position, create new realities within their organization and inspire others to follow. Consider these three examples of change agent leadership:

- Two teachers propose to team teach literacy and inquiry with a looped third and fourth grade class learning math, science, and social studies.
- A principal who is passionate about creating powerful, effective, and joyful Professional Learning Communities in each grade level asks the 6th grade team to work with her to pilot a progress monitoring approach that empowers students to track their own learning and growth.
- A superintendent in a rural school district works with a broad-based community group to develop a vision of an "anytime, anywhere" high school that is able to evolve with emerging and morphing handheld technologies.

The individuals in these three examples hold positions from classroom teacher to superintendent. But, because all of them stepped forward to take the helm of projects that serve their organizations, compel passion and leadership in others, and create new opportunities for stakeholders, each of them exhibits characteristics of transformational leadership.

Transformational leaders seek to make meaningful change that makes a difference over the long haul. These leaders are undaunted by aspirational goals—goals that fix the problems that bedevil the profession, and that create breakthroughs that lead to extraordinary and sustainable results. Unsatisfied with superficial change or change that merely contains a crisis, transformational leaders are as passionate about *how* they achieve remarkable outcomes as they are about the outcomes themselves. They do not agree that the ends justify the means, if the means to those ends diminish people, exclude vulnerable groups of stakeholders, rely on coercion, squelch innovation, or create cumbersome policies and structures that de-energize people (Denning & Dunham, 2010). Transformational leaders exhibit these competencies:

- Employ a coaching leadership style in order to empower and develop leadership in others.
- Articulate a compelling vision that challenges the status quo and inspires others to action.
- Structure meaningful work to create multiple leadership opportunities for others.
- Accomplish change through collaboration and built-up social capital.
- Take a systemic view of change.
- Look for solutions that consider the needs of all, especially those who are most vulnerable.
- Make daily actions consistent with the vision.
- Seek to break through pervasive problems, not just contain a crisis, or manage the status quo.
- Invite experimentation and exploration from others that create radical breakthroughs in paradigms, perspectives, and behavior.
- Tackle aspirational goals, resonate optimism when others think the situation is hopeless, and be resilient in the face of setbacks and disruptions.

FROM TRANSFORMATIONAL LEADERSHIP TO TRANSFORMED ORGANIZATIONS

Transformational change leaders not only influence their colleagues to join them in creating needed change, but also skillfully shepherd the *process* of change around initiatives, thus increasing the learning capacity of the organization. In turn, learning organizations possess the unique ability to sustain and nurture change initiatives and the leaders at their helm.

MIT lecturer and author Peter Senge (1990) is a thought leader on the subject of learning organizations. He describes learning organizations as places "where people continually expand their capacity to create the results they truly desire, where new and expansive patterns of thinking are nurtured, where collective aspiration is set free, and where people are continually learning how to learn together" (p. 3). In the preface of his 2005 book, *Presence: An Exploration of Profound Change in People, Organizations, and Society*, Senge and his co-authors eloquently refer to the interrelationship between parts and the whole, an idea that applies to the synergy between change leaders and the process of change. They write: "It's common to say that trees come from seeds. But, how could a tiny seed create a huge tree? Seeds do not contain the resources needed to grow a tree. These must come from the medium or environment within which the tree grows" (Senge, Scharmer, Jaworski, & Flowers, 2005, p. 2).

Organizations with a deep capacity for change take a resilient stance in response to the messiness of change. They create hospitable conditions for innovate change work to succeed. To the extent that an organization views itself as a learning organization, change work either succeeds or fails. Fullan (2001a) concurs. He writes, "Working through the complexities of change until we get shared meaning and commitment is the only way to get substantial improvement" (p. 272).

WHAT IF YOUR LEADERSHIP COACHING INITIATIVE PLAYED A BIGGER GAME?

Transformational leadership coaching seeks to create long-term, systemic, and sustainable change—the kind of change that develops leaders, teams, and cultures. It asks leaders and coaches to play a bigger game, way beyond managing the status quo. This may sound like a tall order, but why squander resources and energy on leadership coaching that lacks a long-term and systemic impact? Why not wire your coaching strategy for transformational change?

Figure 1.1 is a bulleted list that focuses on the process of transformational leadership coaching. Use the ideas in Figure 1.1 to prompt conversations about leadership coaching in your organization.

Figure 1.1 Wired for Transformational Change

Our leadership coaching program is wired for transformational change because

- It is founded on the belief that leaders come to coaching with wisdom and experience about their work.
- It begins with the passions of coachees and the sense of purpose that comes from being a member of the organization.
- It views events that occur during the change process as opportunities to learn.
- It helps coachees mobilize the process of change surrounding the initiatives they launch.
- It supports coachees in building social capital and in building leadership capacity in others.
- It brings a systemic view to the conversation, helping coachees develop awareness of the whole and create conditions for change.
- It helps coachees deepen their leadership skills as a simultaneous by-product of performing meaningful work.
- It employs processes that awaken coachees to what is possible, and to what has been holding them back.

When leadership coaching is grounded in ideas that arise from what we know about transformational change, it promises to support leaders who seek to go beyond managing the status quo, to create organizations where more people leverage their energy for meaningful change.

Coach More,
Lead More

chapter 2

Leaders don't create followers, they create more leaders.

—Tom Peters (Fast Company online http://www.fastcompany
.com/magazine/44/march-2001)

In a review of research about the ways that leadership influences student learning, commissioned by the Wallace Foundation (Leithwood, Seashore Louis, Anderson, & Wahlstom, 2004), the authors write that especially in underperforming schools, "Leadership is second only to classroom instruction among all school related factors that contribute to what students learn at schools" (p. 5). The authors summarize the core practices of good leadership as the ability to set direction, develop people, and redesign structures in the organization to support rather than hinder successful practices.

The process of transformational leadership coaching promotes all three of these leadership practices. Leaders who coach and coaches who lead have discovered one of the most professionally significant benefits of coaching: *The more you coach, the more you lead—and the more you create other leaders.*

COACHING *IS* LEADERSHIP

Most people would agree with Tom Peters' statement that good leaders do not create followers; they create more leaders. This makes leadership coaching a vital skill for leaders and managers to possess. In their excellent 2002 book, *Execution: The Discipline of Getting Things Done*, Bossidy and Charan agree. They say, "Coaching is the single most important part of expanding others' capabilities . . . [Coaching] is the difference between giving orders and teaching people how to get things done. Good leaders regard every encounter as an opportunity to coach" (p. 74).

Both fledgling and experienced leaders benefit from opportunities to reflect and make decisions in the company of peers and colleagues who help them think, not just provide them with answers. Most of the leaders you coach are sharp thinkers, schooled in the process of change. But, for all they know about *how* to create change, these smart leaders also know that knowing *how* to do something is different from actually *doing it*. Doing it is the hard part. Leadership coaching helps leaders bridge the gaps between wanting to do something to make a difference, knowing how to do it, and actually beginning to do it.

Empowerment

As a leader who wants to be a great coach, you might think that coaching is a simple role to assume. In truth, some leaders find it quite challenging to replace giving answers and advice with the skills of coaching. But, leaders who coach must embrace a definition of leadership as the ability to inspire others to use their talents to lead meaningful work. When they do, they understand that coaching is a demanding measure of leadership.

Coaching is more about empowering other people than dispensing advice and making recommendations. In fact, once they add coaching to their leadership repertoire, many experienced and effective leaders come to the stunning realization that until they stopped having all the answers, they were not really leading at all (Hargrove, 2007).

OPPORTUNITIES FOR LEADERS TO COACH

Schools and districts abound with opportunities to coach. In systems where coaching is a widely accepted practice, individuals in all positions can assume the role of coach: For example, principals coaching teachers as they solve challenges of student learning in the classroom; administrators coaching each other through dilemmas and opportunities; teacher leaders coaching team members; and specialists coaching principals and teachers alike. At the central office level, we see colleagues coaching each other on curriculum projects, and senior leaders coaching each other to make great decisions about policies and procedures.

It Begins With a Conversation

Instilling a culture of coaching within an educational organization often begins with one person's first offer to "coach" another. Consider the following conversation between a principal and a lead teacher where the principal offers coaching in place of advice and answers.

Norah's Story

Norah is an effective and vibrant teacher; her students learn and they love coming to school. For two years, Norah has served as team leader for the fifth grade. In this role, Norah facilitates the Professional Learning Community meetings of the 5th grade teachers. In the first year of leading the PLC, Norah introduced a process for her team to score student work together and track the percentage of students becoming proficient in critical standards. The team even agreed to put a chart up in the hallway so that everyone could see at a glance the growth of the entire grade level. In the first few months after putting up the visual displays of growth data, Norah and her team noticed positive changes in student learning. They were all very excited. It was as if the simple act of tracking data had an impact on student achievement.

The Implementation Dip. But, after six months the data began to level out. Norah knew from her team leader training that the teachers needed to move on from just tracking data, to using the data to identify powerful classroom strategies and interventions to help more students learn at higher levels. Moreover, once they identified the strategies, the teachers needed to actually follow through and apply the strategies with focus and deliberation in their classrooms. They also needed to meet regularly to adjust and revise their use of the strategies in order to keep them vibrant and effective.

Resistance. When Norah shared her observations about this process with the 5th grade team, she met with some resistance that took the form of complaining about the dedicated time necessary for these additional meetings. One influential teacher on the team told Norah,

> Look, what we are doing is already working. The student data show gains—maybe not as fast as we want (or for all students, Norah thought to herself . . .), but gains all the same. We just have to keep going, doing what we each do best in our classrooms. We don't need to meet more often or use the same strategies to be effective.

In Need of Support. Norah felt discouraged by her team's reaction. She began to doubt her ability to serve as team leader. She decided she needed to meet with her principal, Hayden, to ask what she should do to get her team motivated. In the back of her mind, she also thought that maybe it was time to step down as team leader.

Principal Hayden Offers Coaching. Instead of providing Norah with answers and directives about how to work with her team, what if Principal Hayden coached her? What then becomes possible for each fifth grade teacher, for the team, and for Norah as a teacher leader? Let's imagine how Hayden might begin a coaching conversation with Norah:

Norah to her principal:	"Hayden, do you have a minute? I'd like to tell you about a problem I'm having on my grade level team. I just can't get them to follow through and implement the classroom strategies that we agreed to use with our students."
Hayden:	"Norah, now is a great time—I'd be happy to coach you on that."
Norah:	"What do you mean 'coach me'?"
Hayden:	"I listen to you as you tell me about the situation with your team, and then I ask you some questions that help you to think out loud about the details and nuances. I don't give you advice or tell you what you need to do, but I'm certain you'll leave here in twenty minutes with ideas for getting your team to follow through and implement the agreed on classroom strategies."
Norah:	"That sounds good. You're right. What I really want is to understand what I can do to help the team break through this current barrier. It seems so impossible now, but I know other teams are doing it, so we can too!"

In this scenario, Hayden did not have to provide long explanations about what coaching entails; he just needed to recognize that the situation presented by Norah, and Norah's desire to grow as a leader, was a great opportunity for coaching.

On-the-Job Leadership Coaching for Teacher Leaders: The Key to Deep and Sustainable Change

As we see from Norah's story, leadership coaching is a powerful strategy for supporting teacher leaders who are uniquely poised to inspire their colleagues to apply the best practices in curriculum and instruction. When it comes to deep and sustainable implementation of educational strategies, Michael Fullan (2005) writes, "centrally driven reforms can be a necessary first start . . . but can never carry the day of sustainability" (p. 7). The real key to deep implementation and sustainability is when more leaders are willing to take the helm of important initiatives, bring them to life, and then share how they did it with their colleagues. When it comes to initiatives for teaching and learning, no one is better positioned to do this than teachers in the classroom.

TO COACH OR NOT TO COACH

Leaders who coach wear many hats—they are supervisors, mentors, facilitators, collaborators, advice givers, and friends. Since coaching is different from many of these other roles, it is not unusual for leaders to wonder when it is appropriate to coach, and when other forms of leading are more appropriate. Returning to Norah's story, what do you think caused Hayden to offer coaching over other forms of support? Write your thoughts on the lines below:

_____

_____

_____

_____

_____

_____

When to Coach

Fortunately, leaders have ample opportunities to coach the people they lead. But, they have to be on the lookout for these occasions, and then they need to make the simple offer, "may I coach you on this?" Here are a number of conditions when coaching may indeed be the best form of support:

- Coach when individuals and teams have projects in mind, and feel excited about seeing them implemented.
- Coach when individuals and teams come to you with a specific situation or dilemma, and they also have ideas for proactively addressing it. Situations might include preparing for a presentation, setting up an agenda, putting a plan together to carry out an event, or holding a difficult conversation with a co-worker.

- Coach when the development of the individual or team is just as important, if not more important than completing the projects or tasks at hand.
- Coach when individuals or teams are overly dependent on answers and advice from others, and when they lack confidence in their ability to know what to do. Some adults are so afraid of making mistakes that they won't make a move unless the person in charge gives them the green light to proceed. Leaders who offer coaching to these individuals empower them by giving them the experience of discovering their own answers to the dilemmas they face.
- Coach when individuals and teams ultimately need to take responsibility for how their projects turn out, or how situations are addressed and resolved. Through the process of coaching, people come to understand what needs to be done, but also understand how they came to their conclusions. As a result, they can "hold their own," and respond with confidence and insight when called to account for their decisions or propositions.

When Not to Coach

Leaders who coach must also develop a level of discernment that guides them to know when coaching is not the best model for supporting a colleague, or someone they supervise. It is obvious in some situations when coaching is not the appropriate response. These include emergencies, or when an immediate answer is required and time is of the essence. But, other situations are more nuanced and require a contextual decision. For example, some leaders cannot honestly coach when they feel a conflict of interest, such as when they have strong opinions about the coachee's project or plan and what should be done; or they feel there is only one "right" answer; or when they dislike or mistrust the other person. Other times when coaching may or may not be the right response include situations where coachees are new to the requirements of the project and they do not have transferable skills, or when the potential coachee refuses to be coached.

PORTALS TO COACHING

Once you recognize all the opportunities you have in a day to coach, you might also be surprised to learn that leadership coaching is not limited to two people sitting across from each other at a desk. In fact, coaching can occur through several portals, including *Long-Term Leadership Coaching, Just-In-Time Leadership Coaching, Walkabout Leadership Coaching,* and

Leadership Coaching as a Way of Being. Each one of these portals to coaching is described below.

Long-Term Leadership Coaching: A Series of Powerful Coaching Conversations

This book is primarily devoted to teaching long-term coaching, so in this section, I provide just a summary. Long-term leadership coaching is the most comprehensive and formal application of the Flywheel approach to leadership coaching, and it has the potential to create the greatest growth for leaders and their organizations.

In long-term leadership coaching, leaders agree to serve as the designated thought partner for peers and colleagues at the helm of important leadership projects. With a focus on projects that naturally take time to execute, long-term leadership coaching requires leaders to schedule a full complement of coaching sessions, to take place every 7 to 10 days, over a minimum time period of three months. Coaches facilitate this series of conversations using the Powerful Coaching Conversation protocol (see Chapter 5). Leaders who coach individuals long term also ask coachees to sign a coaching agreement (see Chapter 5) and create a First 100-Day Plan to get their project moving and to get the coaching process flowing (see Chapter 4).

Taken to full implementation, long-term leadership coaching demands much of coachees and the leaders who coach them, but also produces tangible rewards for leaders and organizations.

CHARACTERISTICS OF LONG-TERM LEADERSHIP COACHING

1. Occurs through a series of conversations, all focused on accomplishing a specific project coherent to the mission and goals of the organization.

2. A full complement of coaching sessions are scheduled in advance and calendared for at least three months out.

3. Uses a coaching agreement to spell out responsibilities and promises and a First 100-Day Plan to describe the project and get the coaching flowing.

4. Uses the Powerful Coaching Conversation Protocol to guide conversations.

5. Coachee identifies the focus of each session, a specific challenge or opportunity in their project, or with something impeding their progress.

6. Coaching sessions last for 30 to 75 minutes.

7. The coach can be internal or external to the organization.

8. Every conversation begins with accountability and always leads to action.

9. Coaching means coaching: not advising, or providing solutions, or venting, or gossiping and complaining about others.

Just-in-Time Leadership Coaching: A Single Powerful Coaching Conversation

Whereas long-term leadership coaching is a series of conversations, all focused on a meaningful project over at least three months, just-in-time leadership coaching is a single conversation leading to action in a specific challenge or opportunity. Here are a few examples (not an inclusive list!) of what colleagues and peers might ask to be coached on during these single conversations:

- Planning a meeting
- Reflecting on next steps in a process
- Putting together a presentation
- Planning a difficult conversation
- Hammering out a process for collecting data
- Putting together an agenda or syllabus
- Planning an event
- Prioritizing goals and activities
- Designing tools or material
- Setting goals and identifying indicators of success

CHARACTERISTICS OF JUST-IN-TIME LEADERSHIP COACHING

1. Single conversations not necessarily linked to one project.

2. Focuses on meaningful work within the organization.

3. Uses the Powerful Coaching Conversation Protocol to guide conversations.

4. Coachee identifies the focus of each session, a specific challenge or opportunity in a project, or with something impeding progress.

5. Coaching sessions go for 20 to 60 minutes.

6. Can be scheduled in advance or occur spontaneously, if both parties have time.

7. Usually the coach is internal to the organization, but some external coaches offer this service, as well.

8. Always leads to action. The coach follows up with the leader to ask: How did it go?

9. Coaching means coaching: not advising, or providing solutions, or venting, or gossiping and complaining about others.

To further illustrate the "just-in-time" nature of the single coaching conversation, consider this scenario, which is typical in an average week for Dr. Tracee Grigsby-Turner, coordinator of professional development for Alief ISD in Texas. Dr. Grigsby-Turner is well known within her district as a leader who makes herself available to coach. About once or twice per year, Grigsby-Turner agrees to enter into long-term coaching relationships, but more often she provides *Just-in-Time Leadership Coaching.* On almost a daily basis, Grigsby-Turner hears a knock on her office door and finds a colleague standing in the entrance with a perplexed look on his or her face saying something to the effect of, "Hey Tracee, do you have a minute? I'm facing a challenge in my work, and it sure would help if you did that coaching thing you do so I can think this thing through and figure out my next step."

The key to brilliant just-in-time leadership coaching is that just as in long-term leadership coaching, it focuses on important, meaningful work for the leader and the organization. To put it bluntly, just-in-time leadership coaching is not an invitation for griping, gossiping about what other people are doing or not doing, or complaints about work load or people—what leader has time for that? To count as leadership coaching, *just-in-time leadership coaching* must focus on important work, utilize the Powerful Coaching Conversation Protocol, and always lead to action.

In just-in-time leadership coaching, colleagues and peers may not make an appointment with you, or even know to request coaching. As we saw from Grigsby-Turner's experience, colleagues may just show up at your door and inquire, "Do you have a minute?" Leaders who coach learn to love this question because it signals an opportunity to coach.

Walkabout Leadership Coaching

In 2008, I asked three secondary administrators to keep track of the number of people they interact with face-to-face, as they walk about their schools, not including interactions with people in scheduled meetings. These principals told me that on average they had no less than 45 interactions per day. Most of these encounters were of the "do you have a minute?" variety where what transpired were significant, but brief conversations about students, teaching, the curriculum, or the learning environment (Allison, 2008). At the end of our study, the principals wondered how they could use these frequent interactions to build leadership capacity in others.

The answer to this question is found in *Walkabout Leadership Coaching*, the third way that leaders can use leadership coaching to support colleagues and peers. Leaders who engage in walkabout leadership coaching "cherry-pick" coaching skills and strategies in order to

STEPS IN WALKABOUT LEADERSHIP COACHING

1. Stop and acknowledge the person.

2. State how much time you have.

3. Listen.

4. Summarize or paraphrase one crucial point.

5. Leave the coachee with a reflective question.

6. After a day or so, check back with the coachee to ask about results.

make the most of brief, but important interactions with colleagues throughout the normal course of the day.

Some examples of coaching skills and strategies (see Chapters 7 through 10 for details) cherry-picked for the purposes of walkabout leadership coaching include: listening longer than usual and without interruptions, asking one clarifying or detailed question, offering a paraphrase or a summary, or asking a thought leadership question.

Leadership Coaching as a Way of Being

By virtue of its ability to create a fertile coaching culture, the most subtle, yet the most pervasive coaching is *Leadership Coaching as a Way of Being.* Coaching as a way of being embodies Gandhi's encouragement to "Be the change you want to see in the world." As implied by the title, this portal calls on leaders to personify the values and skills of leadership coaching and mindfully act in accordance with them, whenever and wherever they can. For example, leadership coaching thrives in an atmosphere of innovation where "mistakes" are valued for the feedback they provide. Therefore, leaders who coach as a way of being take care to encourage experimentation and resilience in themselves and others, and embrace opportunities to gain wisdom from lessons learned. Both in their professional and personal lives, leaders who coach as a way of being also listen more, refrain from jumping in to solve problems and give advice, and follow through on commitments to others—not just when they are coaching, but in every interaction. The more people in an organization who lead from a coaching perspective, the more the culture of the organization becomes hospitable to coaching. And, a culture that welcomes and supports the practices and values of coaching also sustains coaching as a cultural norm.

ANSWERING THE CALL

To reap the delightful benefits that come from coaching your colleagues and team members, leaders who coach need to do a little soul searching to identify their personal Achilles heel. The following inventory gives you a chance to honestly consider the challenges you might personally face as you move more into the coaching role as a leader. Don't be discouraged, no matter how you score on this inventory! I have seen leaders who thought they could never coach become incredible coaches sought out by colleagues and the people they lead, once they let go of the need to have all the answers, all the time.

Consider the questions provided on the survey below and rate yourself according to the levels provided.

Called to Coaching

The personal inventory presented in Figure 2.1, Called to Coaching, helps leaders assess themselves for accommodating coaching perspectives.

Figure 2.1   Called to Coaching

1. Although I am a leader and am known for my expertise, I do not feel obliged to have all the answers.

   This is not me at all.   This sounds exactly like me.

   1   2   3   4   5   6   7   8   9   10

2. I do not try to have all the answers in order to "look good" to the people around me.

   This is not me at all.   This sounds exactly like me.

   1   2   3   4   5   6   7   8   9   10

3. I am not known as a gossip, nor do I traffic with gossips or offer information about other people in order to be accepted by a group of gossips.

   This is not me at all.   This sounds exactly like me.

   1   2   3   4   5   6   7   8   9   10

4. Even though it would be quicker to solve problems for others, I most often resist doing this and instead help others solve the problems themselves.

   This is not me at all.   This sounds exactly like me.

   1   2   3   4   5   6   7   8   9   10

5. I often know what I think is the right or best answer, but I prefer to bring out expertise in others.

   This is not me at all.   This sounds exactly like me.

   1   2   3   4   5   6   7   8   9   10

6. Leaders exist at all levels in the system, and I believe these individuals have unique wisdom and answers.

   This is not me at all.   This sounds exactly like me.

   1   2   3   4   5   6   7   8   9   10

7. The people I lead (or have led in the past) come up with revisions, refinements, and innovative ideas to further the vision of the organization. I trust the wisdom in others that leads them to these visions.

   This is not me at all.   This sounds exactly like me.

   1   2   3   4   5   6   7   8   9   10

8. I have people in my life who listen to me, and I have experienced firsthand the value of having time to hear my own thoughts.

   This is not me at all.   This sounds exactly like me.

   1   2   3   4   5   6   7   8   9   10

9. I have tackled difficult projects in my own life and work, and have successfully taken action to bring about change or create something meaningful.

   This is not me at all.   This sounds exactly like me.

   1   2   3   4   5   6   7   8   9   10

10. I do not have a need to "save" other people from the discomfort of their struggles and experiences.

    This is not me at all.   This sounds exactly like me.

    1   2   3   4   5   6   7   8   9   10

This tool is also available for download at www.WisdomOut.com and www.Corwin.com/Flywheel.

Reflecting on Your Inventory Results

If you have been honest about your ratings, you probably wrestled with at least one of the ideas presented in the survey. This does not mean that you cannot learn to be a great coach. What it does mean is that you need to raise your awareness about these ideas and notice how they influence the way you interact with others and engage with your own work.

Strategies for working on the areas you scored with an 8 or below:

1. Write the statements on sticky notes. For as many weeks as it takes, pick a statement to focus on, and carry that statement with you for a day or more. Notice what it takes for you to move higher on the scale.

2. Share your challenge areas with a colleague and ask them to watch you for a few days as you focus your thoughts, emotions, and behaviors on a particular statement from the sticky notes. Ask them to give you feedback about what they notice.

3. Additionally, if you have yet to work with a coach to accomplish an important project on your plate, now would be a good time to engage the services of one. Working with a great coach requires you to experience firsthand what it is to be a coachee. Once you walk in the coachee's shoes and experiences, you acquire a sincere level of compassion and authenticity that cannot be learned by reading a book.

ON TO PART II!

Part II of this book is called *Projects*, and describes the transformational change work most worthy of leadership coaching. In Chapter 3, you learn how to help leaders identify projects that have the potential to change education for a greater good. Chapter 4 provides ideas and tools for you to use to inspire leaders to get their projects moving in the first 100 days.

Part II

Projects

The Greater Good

What Leaders Want You to Coach Them On

chapter 3

Start something that matters.

—Blake Mycoskie *(Start Something That Matters*, 2011*)*

When I speak about leadership for a greater good, a lot of people immediately conjure up images of Gandhi, Mother Teresa, Martin Luther King, and César Chávez—wise leaders associated with social activism and global change. Wisdom is a daunting concept to many. As such, many people believe it is a characteristic reserved for iconic leaders throughout time, unattainable to regular people like us, who wake up many mornings feeling more like Homer Simpson than the Dalai Lama. Yet, to deprive ourselves of wisdom is to deprive ourselves of a really great way of living in the world, a way that employs meaningful work and meaningful endeavors to shape life toward a greater good.

As a leadership coach, you have the opportunity to support leaders in long-term projects (in addition to *Just-in-Time Coaching*, and *Walkabout Coaching*—as described in Chapter 2) as they take action toward accomplishing meaningful work. But, some of the leaders you coach do not instinctively know how to define or redefine their work in ways that help the organization accomplish aspirational goals. Or, they may feel inspired by their work, but do not think of it as being meaningful to others or to the system, and therefore have not leveraged their energy for breakthrough results. As a coaching leader, you have a responsibility to help others either recognize *how* their work is meaningful, or to help them reconfigure their work so that it *becomes* meaningful.

To help you fulfill this responsibility, this chapter explains projects and what it means to use them in service of the greater good. Then, you learn about practical tools you can use during initial meetings with the leaders you coach, to help them discover and articulate a project for coaching.

PROJECTS

Projects are how leaders get things done (Kouzes & Pozner, 2003). And so it follows that long-term transformational leadership coaching—coaching with the goal of supporting leaders who want to make meaningful change—focuses on projects. Projects are complex, and therefore they provide realistic, practical backdrops for the leaders you coach to test their mettle, and learn new leadership skills. Projects demand actions that in turn lead to implementation within the organization. And because they have a beginning, middle, and end projects necessitate timelines, needed resources, and the engagement of colleagues. Projects also focus the coaching process; they provide important and compelling reasons for leaders to make coaching sessions a priority. Most importantly, projects create new, renewed, or reengineered practices, structures, policies, and products within the organization—hopefully to eliminate barriers, not to create more complexity and hoops for people to jump through. In other words, *projects make organizational change visible.*

The Relevance of Projects to Coaching Conversations

Coaching is always about action and change. In the absence of projects, long-term leadership coaching becomes a series of unrelated "chats," which at their worst devolve into laments about the "problem of the day" and at their best, are simply theoretical musings that rarely lead to action, or produce visible outcomes in the organization. As one leadership coach told me, "Without projects, it is hard to imagine what you would coach a person on long term."

Some leaders like the idea of working with a leadership coach, but they balk at focusing the coaching on challenging leadership projects. Leaders who resist setting up a project to focus their coaching may be confused about what it means to have a leadership coach. They may mistakenly believe the role of the coach is to provide advice, counseling, or information. Leaders who ask you to coach them long term, but who stop short of setting up a project may try to persuade you to leave coaching conversations "open" to whatever comes up, to the problem *du jour*—whatever seems most pressing at the moment. But, the "let's not have a project" approach is a sure way to seriously undermine one of the most powerful outcomes of long-term coaching: accomplishing something important to improve the organization (Allison & Reeves, 2012).

Coaching is an expensive proposition if leaders only want to be coached on tasks that do not create value or contribute to the mission of the organization. Leaders who understand the power of coaching *want* to focus on challenging projects knowing that coaching provides an advantage, and if coaching were not available, the project would suffer or even fail.

What Makes a Project?

Projects worthy of coaching possess fundamental qualities that add value to leaders and organizations. Specifically,

- they are visible and tangible. They produce something new or different or they evolve an existing initiative or focus in the system;
- they show clear value toward advancing the mission of the organization and create coherence rather than imposing a burden or fragmentation (Fullan, 2002);
- they can be led by leaders, through their positions in the organization. Projects certainly need to be aspirational, but they also need to fall within your coachee's circle of influence and accountability. Coachees must be self-empowered to take action within their project, either with others or through others;
- they are complex. Other leaders through different positions in the system may be working on projects to contribute to the accomplishment of the same goal;
- they can be monitored for implementation (which shows that the project is moving forward) and effectiveness (which shows that the project is having an impact), both in the short term and long term;
- they have start dates and due dates, in between are ranges where milestones are met and demonstrate that the project is moving forward;
- they require the involvement of other people in the system who become engaged through *their* roles at different stages of the project to help launch, implement, support, and evaluate the project;
- they roll out research-based strategies and initiatives that implement the best of what works in education, while simultaneously inviting innovation, creativity, action research, and an entrepreneurial spirit;
- they stretch your coachees as leaders, projects are more than tasks on a "to do" list;
- they produce insights about leadership that are pertinent to other important projects your coachees lead (Goldsmith & Reiter, 2007);
- they develop the leadership abilities of others and extend leadership opportunities to them; and
- they produce learning for the organization and answer questions about how the organization learned.

Before you read the next section, go back to Chapter 1 and compare the characteristics of projects to the characteristics of transformational leadership.

What do you notice? How does the concept of "project" as described in this chapter connect with the principles of transformational leadership?

THE GREATER GOOD

Long-term leadership coaching requires that leaders and coaches invest valuable energy and time in holding powerful coaching conversations. It also requires organizations to make investments in teaching leaders how to effectively coach their colleagues and peers. Given the investment of resources, time, and energy, the gains from transformational leadership coaching are fully realized through projects that demand much more than the accomplishment of daily tasks or maintenance of the status quo. After all, why squander powerful leadership coaching on work that does not make a significant, positive difference?

The Greater Good Defined

Although Flywheel Leadership Coaching certainly produces short-term benefits and personal pride, the real goal for the leaders you coach is to catalyze their ability to create lasting positive change through projects that serve a greater good over "business as usual." Projects that serve a greater good are complex. They bring people, skills, knowledge, and resources together to create value that transcends any single person or organizational set of needs in order to benefit all stakeholders and society, today and into the future. These projects often call long-standing cultural norms and organizational practices into question. Indeed, to serve a greater good, leadership projects concern themselves with improving the system surrounding important work—a necessary consideration for sustainable change. These projects can even make a historical difference in the field of education, or fulfill a personal legacy (Fink & Hargreaves, 2006).

In order to create movement toward the greater good, educational leaders must take actions in the present moment with awareness of the downstream effect of those actions and the likely future result of their accumulated impact. The question for today's educational leaders is this: *how do you create organizations that are efficient and effective in the short term (students mastering important standards, for example) that are also resilient and relevant over the long haul (for example, developing awesome young people who self-actualize and make a difference in an ever-changing world)?*

Wisdom and the Greater Good

Serving the *greater good* originates in long-standing ideas about what it means to be wise, and has always provided a strong pull to humankind to commit to meaningful and challenging work that makes the world a better place (Kilburg, 2006).

Past president of the American Psychological Association Robert Sternberg is a leading expert and prolific writer on the topic of wisdom. Sternberg puts forth what he calls the *Balance Theory of Wisdom* (2000) and associates wisdom with what he calls the *common good*, and what I call the *greater good*.

Sternberg writes "Wisdom is defined as the application of successful intelligence and creativity as mediated by values toward the achievement of a common good" (2000, p. 152).

Before Sternberg, Abraham Maslow also associated the greater good with people who take action while considering the needs of others. As I was doing the research for this book, I was intrigued to learn that Maslow wrote about a concept he called "transcendence of the ego," which like Sternberg's balance theory of wisdom also refers to motivation kindled by the human impulse to serve a greater good. As you might remember from your "Intro to Psych" class, most published depictions of Maslow's 1943 Hierarchy of Needs pyramid place "Self Actualization" as the highest form of motivation for human beings. However, in later writings Maslow described a sixth motivational level of *Self-Transcendence* as the pinnacle of his famous pyramid (Koltko-Rivera, 2006). In his personal journals and in an article he published in the *Journal of Transpersonal Psychology* in 1969, Maslow put forth the idea that people who operate at the level of self-transcendence "seek to serve a cause beyond oneself which may include service to others or devotion to an ideal" (Koltko-Rivera, 2006, p. 303).

Other authorities urge leaders to transform their management and engagement style in order to catalyze or inspire the greater good throughout their organizations. Leading educator Michael Fullan consistently urges leaders to make a difference in the lives of students by embracing moral purpose, which he describes as being socially responsible to others and to the environment. From Fullan's perspective, moral purpose demands that leaders concern themselves with the bigger picture, not just with performance improvement for their own schools, but also for every other school in the system. Leaders with moral purpose also seek to develop and deepen leadership in others and throughout the organization (Fullan, 2002). Likewise, in his 2009 *Harvard Business Review* article "Moonshots for Management," Gary Hamel writes that a primary leadership challenge is to orient itself to achievement of noble and socially significant goals by ensuring that managerial work "serves a higher purpose" (p. 2). And, in his terrific book titled *Drive: The Surprising Truth About What Motivates Us*, Daniel Pink writes, "The most deeply motivated people—not to mention those who are most productive and satisfied—hitch their desires to a cause larger than themselves" (p. 133).

The nature of wisdom in individuals may be difficult to describe, but leadership wisdom is usually recognized in people who respond to big challenges, dilemmas, and adversities by creating solutions and making decisions that are good for people and organizations alike. Thus, the pursuit of wisdom through serving a greater good fits perfectly with models of transformational coaching, which always supports leaders as they achieve remarkable results.

The Greater Good in Action

To return to Maslow's revised hierarchy, when physiological and safety needs are met, people are motivated to action not by the rewards that come from incentives, pay, company swag, slogans, or short-term gains, but by contributing to the well-being of others. And, because the impulse to serve the greater good through meaningful work is a powerful vehicle that moves people from compliant engagement to authentic engagement—and truly is a source of professional joy—then serving a greater good is good for individuals *and* for organizations (Moss-Kanter, 2010).

In helping professions, such as education, it is assumed that everyone in the system is focused on the greater good. After all, aren't we all here for the betterment of the students? Although most educators care deeply about their students, they can also fall prey to exhaustion, disenchantment, unrest, depression, and disillusionment about their work. Dissonant states of being cause some educators to cut corners, withdraw, fail to collaborate, retreat into cliques, lash out at groups they disagree with, seek the comfort of the status quo, and actively resist progress. Others develop leadership blind spots that prevent them from seeing how they could do more or how their leadership style is turning a well-intended and promising initiative into something that chips away at people and the culture (Frost, 2002). Still, other educators succumb to a management style more concerned with preserving rules and regulations that inhibit innovation and engagement; or worse yet, they create what I call "Rube Goldberg-like" procedures that build in complexities, lack focus, and defy common sense (Allison & Reeves, 2012; Hess, 2010). For example, an educator I know in a large school district in a southern state was told to quit using a reading strategy he honed through experimentation and experience in the classroom, because it "wasn't on the list of approved strategies"—even though it helped scores of struggling kindergarten students finally grasp letter sounds. Educators who create dissonance have lost their passion, and are operating either in a mode of grim determination, or open hostility. They are not thinking of the greater good. Nevertheless, given the strength of the human desire to make a difference for others, the possibility that any leader at any time could provoke action toward the greater good is very strong.

So what does it look like when educators work toward a greater good? I frequently think of Alonzo, a teacher leader in Houston whose coaching project for the greater good was to reorganize the science lab supply room as a way to reduce stress for his colleagues, and ensure that they would use the supplies to create inspiring learning experiences for students. What made Alonzo's project stunningly wise and effective involved the metrics he used to measure its success: The percentage of science teachers whose lessons were well-designed was determined by a rubric where proficiency entailed, using the lab materials that were available in Alonzo's well-organized supply room. Some might look at Alonzo's project and decide it falls short of serving the greater good—it just isn't fancy enough, or big enough, or bold enough. But, when you recall Schmoker's call for focus on well-designed lessons as a strategy for closing achievement gaps (see the Preface), you realize Alonzo *is* taking action toward the greater good, applying his power and influence through his current role and the work he has chosen to do. The reorganization of the science supply room is Alonzo's piece of the "greater good" pie. And, as Alonzo carries out this project, he simultaneously develops leadership competencies—such as resilience, communicating his vision and progress, linking it to research, measuring outcomes, motivating others—that prime him to take on even bigger projects. Leadership coaching is one way to help leaders like Alonzo perform real work that makes a difference while evolving their leadership.

As we see from Alonzo's project, the greater good is often brought about through humble action passionately trained on the most complex of problems. In fact, the more complex the problem, the more opportunity there is to do something about it from many different angles. Complexity is really opportunity for the greater good. In Table 3.1, by comparing the greater good to business as usual, we further illuminate how the leaders you coach can have a profound impact on their organization, and why projects for the greater good are the perfect context for leadership coaching.

HELPING LEADERS SELECT COACHING PROJECTS

Before you begin the series of coaching conversations that characterize long-term leadership coaching, you meet with your coachees to clarify what they want you to coach them on, framed as a project for the greater good. As I wrote at the start of this chapter, some leaders instinctively know the areas where they want coaching. Others benefit from you using the tools provided here, to guide them toward their projects. Figure 3.1 offers a process for your coachees to vet potential projects.

Table 3.1 The Greater Good Versus Business as Usual

The Greater Good	Business as Usual
• Is inclusive: Seeks to create benefits for all students, the high achievers AND the most vulnerable whose success is in jeopardy	• Is exclusive: Creates benefits for the best and brightest students (who are likely to succeed under any conditions)
• Seeks to create important, needed, and meaningful change in order to benefit many people and the surrounding context	• Seeks to maintain comfort and the status quo for a few people
• Is a by-product of many people tackling complex, persistent, and vexing problems from different angles	• Complex problems are seen as being too messy, too wicked to do anything about
• Considers the impact on future generations for the long term and builds in safeguards to minimize unintentional consequences	• Serves the short-term needs only of current stakeholders and often the most influential and privileged
• Is made visible through action taken by those who see the need for change	• The current status quo prevails, characterized by a lack of action
• Is brought about by individuals seeking real accomplishment and humbly accepting accolades as by-products of meaningful work	• Leaders seek accolades for personal effort as the main reason for taking on important projects
• Arises out of processes that align with the outcomes: "Means are not justified by the ends"	• The end is justified by any means, such as questionable processes (e.g., fudging the data), coercion, or limiting opportunities for others
• Is coherent to the mission and highest purpose of the organization	• People feel a lack of coherence between initiatives and the mission of the organization and are overwhelmed by competing initiatives and pet projects
• Creates and opens up leadership opportunities for others	• Involves only the "usual suspects" and maintains leadership roles only for those who already have it
• Simultaneously transforms the culture surrounding the initiative, in order to create partnerships that empower people to renew and therefore sustain the initiative	• Ignores the culture surrounding the initiative, decreasing the likelihood of renewal and sustainability
• Is often fueled by personal passion that begs to manifest through the role of leaders	• Conforms to existing expectations and paralyzes innovation

Figure 3.1 A Process to Vet Projects for Flywheel Leadership Coaching

Directions: Use the worksheet below to help the leaders you coach select their coaching projects.

Step 1. First list titles for the top five meaningful work projects that you lead or could lead, given your position in the organization and your personal passions. These projects could already be on your plate, or they could be projects that need to be started or revived, or they could be something you have been longing to do because you know they would be good for people and for the organization. These projects might advance new initiatives or they might refine, revise, or deepen existing initiatives.

Title your top five project possibilities and list them here:

Project Possibility 1: _____

Project Possibility 2: _____

Project Possibility 3: _____

Project Possibility 4: _____

Project Possibility 5: _____

Step 2. Now, copy the table below for each project possibility you listed above and write the project title on the top line. With that project in mind, assign a number (1–5) with 1 indicating the lowest presence of the quality for a greater good and 5 indicating the highest amount of the quality for a greater good, for each item listed in the table below. The highest score a project can receive is 45. The closer a project is to the score of 45, the more likely it is to produce results for a greater good.

Vetting Process

Project Possibility Title: _____

Project Qualities for a Greater Good. The extent to which this project:						
1. Is something I feel personally passionate about and can begin now.	2. Aligns with and is coherent with the goals of the organization and serves to advance the mission.	3. Builds leadership in others and gives them opportunities to lead.	4. Seeks to create solutions to vexing problems in my organization and/or the greater field of education.	5. Mobilizes the best of what we know about great teaching, learning, and leadership.	6. Is something I can lead through the influence and work of my role and reputation.	7. Will ultimately create benefits for all students and stakeholders, especially those who are most vulnerable.
1–5	1–5	1–5	1–5	1–5	1–5	1–5	TOTAL SCORE
Your Score:	Your Score:	Your Score:	Your Score:	Your Score:	Your Score:	Your Score:	
Notes and Reflection:	Notes and Reflection:	Notes and Reflection:	Notes and Reflection:	Notes and Reflection:	Notes and Reflection:	Notes and Reflection:	

This tool is also available for download at www.WisdomOut.com and www.Corwin.com/Flywheel.

WHAT COULD YOU BE COACHED ON?

Leaders who coach—leaders like you—wouldn't think of asking colleagues and peers to do something they are not willing to do themselves. For this reason, the best coaches are those who have experienced coaching. Before you begin coaching other leaders, I urge you to first develop your own project and find someone to coach you on it. Through the experience of being coached, you develop tremendous compassion for the individuals you coach. You wrestle with quandaries and dilemmas, make tough decisions, confront "push back" from those who prefer the status quo over needed change, and develop resilience in order to bounce forward during times of challenge.

In this chapter, you picked up ideas and tools about how to help the leaders you coach focus on projects that go big and serve a greater good. In the next chapter, you learn how to help the leaders you coach take action on these projects within the first 100 days.

ADDITIONAL TOOLS RELATED TO THIS CHAPTER

Bringing Out the Best: Questions Coaches Can Ask to Help Leaders Think About the Greater Good

- What is the greatest need in your organization and what is most powerful thing you could do?
- Where do you see the work of your position bringing out the best in the mission of this organization?
- What feels very difficult to you, but seems necessary to right a wrong, or create something better for employees or stakeholders?
- How do the challenges and adversities of your life provide ideas for what to do?
- How does your current project measure in order to impact a larger group of people, or the planet, or future generations?
- If you accomplished your project, what are you facing that would make you feel excited, proud?
- What do you want to accomplish that would define you as a leader?
- If you could leave a legacy, what would it be?

This tool is also available for download at www.WisdomOut.com and www.Corwin.com/Flywheel.

The First
100 Days

chapter 4

Let us watch well our beginnings and results will manage themselves.

—Alexander Clark (American Clergyman, 1834–1879)

In 2009, while attending a conference in Florida, I had the opportunity to witness a NASA space shuttle launch from Cape Canaveral. It was early evening and I joined a crowd of other enthusiastic conference goers in the courtyard of the restaurant where we had just finished dinner. Scanning the twilight sky, eager to catch the first glimpse of light from the rocket, I couldn't help but think anxiously of the Challenger's failed lift-off in 1986, and the loss of seven lives, including teacher Christa McAuliffe. On this night, I urged the shuttle and its seven-person crew forward: keep going, keep going, keep going, I whispered toward the sky. I knew that a good launch was absolutely essential to the success of this shuttle. Without a successful lift-off, facilitated by the powerful booster rocket, the shuttle would never make it into space, let alone complete its journey. Luckily, I had a camera with me and was able to snap several pictures in a row, capturing the exact moment when the booster engine fell away from the body of the shuttle, curved, and dropped down into the sea. Finally, I took a breath; the launch was a success. And, although a long journey remained, and malfunctions and missteps could surely still befall it, this shuttle was off to a good start.

WHAT'S SO BIG ABOUT THE FIRST 100 DAYS?

I offer my space shuttle story to provide you with a metaphor to use in your work as a leadership coach: the First 100-Day Plan is a rocket booster that launches the leadership projects you are coaching. And, a good launch is essential to successful implementation and visible results.

Given the high rate of plan failures (including those promising needed change), it is surprising that many leaders (in all industries—not just education) appear unaware that there even exists a systematic approach for initiating projects (Daly & Watkins, 2006). Lacking knowledge about how to initiate change makes leaders unfocused and clumsy in their approach. Some do not take action at all, or fetter away their time and energy on managing the status quo. Others jump ahead too fast, expecting implementation before people and systems are ready.

The Power of a Good Launch

So what's so big about the first 100 days? The bottom line is this: botched beginnings create resistance to change. And, resistance in the early phases of a change effort jeopardizes the subsequent phases of implementation and continuation (Fullan, 1991). When you consider that 100 days is one quarter, or more than three months, 2,400 hours or 14,400 minutes, perhaps the bigger question is this: why would *any* leader, but especially those who are passionate about making a positive and lasting difference for the greater good, squander 100 days? The First 100-Day Plan is a tool that makes the initiation phase visible and deliberate. It mitigates the challenges of change and thus reduces resistance.

What we know about resistance necessarily takes us back to a fundamental reality of life: change is hard. Indeed, the initial stage of any change process competes against the compelling pull of the past—the gravity of nostalgia—and the love affair that people and complex systems alike seem to have with the comforts of the status quo (Hamel, 2009). Michael Fullan (2002) calls this the implementation gap and he wisely counsels leaders not to underestimate it. He says, "Leaders can't avoid the inevitable early difficulties of trying something new. They should know for example, that no matter how much they plan for the change, the first six months or so of implementation will be bumpy" (p. 18). Given that even the best laid plans can go awry, it pays for leaders to understand how to bank change initiatives toward successful implementation.

**A Powerful Coaching Tool: The Relevancy of
First 100-Day Plans to Coaching**

As a leadership coach, there is another benefit that makes first 100-day planning absolutely essential to your work. When combined with leadership coaching, it amplifies the coaching process, and positions you to skillfully create conversations for your coachees to focus on the actions that will make them successful. First 100-Day Plans are relevant to long-term leadership coaching in at least six important ways:

1. They get the coaching process flowing, right from the start. The First 100-Day Plan truly answers the question: *What do you want me to coach you on?*

2. They create momentum and sustain the coaching process. As the First 100-Day Plan unfolds, and your coachees take action in the real world, events are triggered that produce new results, new dilemmas, new challenges, and new opportunities that shape the purpose of coaching and create momentum within the coaching process.

3. They build strong and trustworthy coaching relationships. There is nothing more powerful for creating strong relationships than learning how to face challenges together.

4. They make the value of leadership coaching visible, and therefore measurable right from the start during the initiation phase of the transformational change process—a vulnerable time when many change efforts fail.

5. During coaching conversations, they operate as companion tools to the Powerful Coaching Conversation Protocol. They help to focus the conversation.

6. They create a record of intentions, and call your coachees to action that maintains an intense focus on the advancement of their projects.

In this book you find many practical tools for enhancing your work as a leadership coach. When it comes to long-term leadership coaching, the First 100-Day Plan readily proves its value.

THE FIRST 100-DAY PLAN DEFINED

The First 100-Day Plan is a set of strategic actions taken by individuals who feel called to *lead*; to start or revitalize initiatives that serve the goals and mission of their organizations. The First 100-Day Plan template inspires leaders to set projects up for success with fifteen essential prompts

Here are just a few examples of the projects I've seen leaders take on over the last decade:

- The assistant superintendent who redesigned the teacher induction program to include action research projects in partnership with mentor teachers.
- The high school social studies teacher who persuaded two of his colleagues to join him by using writing rubrics to give students feedback on their essays.
- The principal who created a cadre of leadership coaches in her school, composed of administrators and grade-level teacher team leaders.
- The Human Resources (HR) director who put herself at the helm of a huge initiative to link the administrator evaluation system to national leadership standards.
- The superintendent who set out to make his district a leader in 21st century learning.
- The crossing guard supervisor who put together a booklet and workshop called "Ten Powerful Things to Say to Kids to Help Them Start the Day Right" as a strategy for improving community relationships.
- The 5th grade teacher who started a school newspaper to provide a real-world application for students to practice and improve nonfiction writing, and to involve more students in school activities.
- The assistant principal who created a fun and easy data system to track reading progress for kindergarten teachers and their students.
- The school police officer who started the anti-bully club in his assigned school.
- The technology specialist who started a computer class for parents in the community without access to technology at home.
- The English as a Second Language (ESL) teacher who mobilized a volunteer weekend field-trip program for students of families recently immigrated to the United States, who did not have a car to transport their kids to the great museums and events in the surrounding area.

or calls to action. These actions not only increase acceptance for the initiative early on, but also create conditions in the system that strengthen the implementation and continuation phases.

High Impact Actions

A quick check of the online Encarta World English Dictionary (1999) offers several definitions of the word "initiative," the second of which says that it is "the first step in a process that once taken determines subsequent events." Certain high-powered actions are critical to the success of your project, and leaders should apply them to the specific details of the first 100 days of any change initiative they lead.

The First 100-Day Plan Template

Table 4.1 presents the First 100-Day Plan template and summarizes the three phases and the actions taken in each. Immediately following the template, you find a more detailed description of the actions in each phase. When you work with the leaders you coach, ask them to read these descriptions and keep them handy as they write up the specific actions they decide to take to initiate their project.

DESCRIPTIONS OF THE ACTIONS IN EACH PHASE

Phase I. The First 33 Days: Build Excitement, Interest, Knowledge, and Demonstrate Systemic Coherence

1. **Use data to demonstrate the urgency and relevancy of your project and motivate support.** Persuading others to support initiatives requires change leaders to assemble existing data found within the system, combine it with external data and research, and use it to present a compelling case for change. In his 2007 article for *Harvard Business Review*, "Leading Change: Why Transformation Efforts Fail," change guru John Kotter writes, "This first step is essential because just getting a transformation program started requires the aggressive cooperation of many individuals. Without motivation, people won't help and the effort goes nowhere" (p. 98).

2. **Articulate how the initiative you want to lead is coherent to the mission, vision, and goals of the organization. Be on the lookout for key colleagues who "get your vision" and who are eager and interested.** Many systems come preloaded (if you'll permit me to use a computer metaphor) with well-articulated visions, missions, purposes, and imperatives, and the leaders you coach need to link their projects and initiatives to them. Michael Fullan calls this "coherence making" (Fullan, 2001a, 2002). Because coherence making battles the inherent tendency of complex systems to generate overload and fragmentation, it increases buy-in and reduces resistance.

3. **Secure the First Followers (invite, identify, entice, recruit, persuade, look for volunteers).** These are the people and teams eager to pilot the initiative, test theories, and experiment to seek breakthrough results. They improve on it by working out the kinks, and by discovering what the initiative needs in order to work in real-world settings. The enthusiasm of the First Followers makes the innovation enticing to others. The First Followers make your coachee's vision more visible.

4. **Assemble a lead team of rapid responders.** Think of this group as your coachee's advisory team, change champions, or guiding coalition. This

team understands the project and how it advances the mission of the organization. This is a team that can and will rapidly respond to requests for support, resources, feedback, and ideas. Ideally, this team knows the project well enough that they can accurately represent it to others in the system who are concerned about it, or who are just learning about it and have questions.

5. Plan and provide professional development for the First Followers. Identify the learning needs of the First Followers and put together a professional development plan with initial learning experiences that can get underway immediately.

Phase II. The Second 33 Days: Metrics, Pilot, Innovate, Tinker, Insight, Communicate

1. Select and articulate to others a few meaningful metrics to track the impact of your project. Set up a system or dashboard that is easily updated and shared (if you need assistance, enlist the help of someone good at this).

2. Refine and continue professional development for the First Followers and extend learning opportunities to others. Conduct a second needs assessment of the First Followers and provide quality professional development as needed. Don't wait for perfection before you empower First Followers to begin; First Followers often simultaneously learn, and experiment, and apply.

3. Empower the First Followers to get going with the initiative and support them like crazy! Rapidly respond to the First Followers about whatever comes up for them, preferably in person. When they want to experiment, be certain to communicate with them, extend gratitude, and provide support. Mitigate the stresses of change where you can (e.g., reduce other commitments, provide great professional development) without backing away from action, and make requests to the lead team to remove barriers and open doors.

4. Recognize breakthrough practices and surprising tactics taken by the First Followers that create the greatest gains. Learn from the First Followers exactly what they are discovering about carrying out the initiative.

For example, one leadership coach told me about a teacher leader named Christopher who implemented a new program of using writing prompts. While rolling out the writing prompts, Christopher and his teammates discovered that students write more coherent paragraphs when they first use sticky notes to organize and reorganize their outlines. They further discovered that after they reorganize their sticky notes, students write more efficiently, if they explain their reasons for doing so to a learning buddy. Although the sticky notes were not prescribed in the official initiative process, they did not undermine the integrity of the process; therefore, Christopher and his team felt free to use them. Not wanting to keep this discovery to themselves, they wrote a one-page description and videotaped students willing to demonstrate. Christopher then shared the video footage at a district curriculum development meeting where more colleagues learned the adaptation, too.

5. Provide opportunities and forums for the First Followers and the lead team to tell the story about how the project is proceeding. This action not only communicates the change initiative, but also perhaps at this point, it more importantly gives First Followers and lead team members visibility and credibility as coleaders of the initiative.

Phase III. The Third 33 Days: Celebrate Early Wins and Favorite Mistakes, Revise and Refine, Deepen the Movement, Secure Support, and Remove Barriers

1. Broadcast and celebrate small wins (any movement toward achieving milestones) and favorite mistakes (where you learned the most). Harvard Business School Researchers Teresa Amabile and Steven Kramer found that when it comes to change projects, small wins recognized regularly confirm for people that they are making progress on meaningful work (Amabile & Kramer, 2011). Small wins are anything you want to see more of: more teachers trained, more principals using a new skill, more classrooms engaged, and more students learning.

In addition to celebrating small wins, I'm a big proponent of celebrating the learning that comes out of missteps and mistakes—what I call "favorite mistakes." Leaders who celebrate favorite mistakes do more than increase organizational learning; they also steer the culture toward accepting the idea that "mistakes" produce the most profound learning, and ought to be mined for the pearls of wisdom they contain.

Use the knowledge gained both from small wins and favorite mistakes to decide those elements which merit continued commitment, and those areas requiring mid-course corrections. Then, revise tactics, resources, structures, processes, and tools accordingly. Document the revisions for the next wave of participants.

2. Identify the next wave of participants who can implement and lead the vision, and plan professional development. Use the National Professional Development Standards published by Learning Forward to design a quality program for stakeholders involved in the change initiative. Cast the First Followers in leadership roles in this effort, as mentors, coaches, and models.

3. Define new goals, identify milestones for the next 12 months (after the first 100 days), and establish the system for monitoring and reporting indicators. Using what you learned from the First Followers, establish goals for the initiative to move into deeper implementation. Select just two to three metrics to track movement toward the goals.

4. Gain audiences with decision makers and internal and external stakeholders to overcommunicate knowledge and information. Leaders of change initiatives need to overcommunicate or reiterate their direction in more than one way, at more than one time, and using every outlet available. Communication examples include: newsletters, blogs, Question & Answer sessions, presentations, meetings, one-on-one conversations, course offerings, workshops, and speakers, to name just a few.

5. Remove or revise systems, structures, policies, and practices undermining the vision. As more people in the organization become involved in change initiatives, more obstacles preventing forward motion are likely to appear. Frequently these obstacles have to do with issues related to time—usually not having enough of it. But, they also have to do with team configurations, job descriptions, grant requirements, hierarchical expectations, evaluation programs, and physical space configurations—the list could go on and on (Ashkenas, 2010). This review and revision requires leaders to work closely with their leadership/advisory team who have hopefully been kept apprised of these barriers, and can now advocate for their removal or reduction.

FINAL GUIDELINES

As a practicing leadership coach as well as a trainer and mentor of leadership coaches, I subject myself to using the same tools and processes that I present to you in this book—at times, especially with the earliest versions, to my extreme mortification. Moved to action by these experiences, I have reengineered, revised, tinkered with and revamped multiple iterations of each tool and process proposed here. The First 100-Day Plan in this chapter has been used by hundreds of leadership coaches, and their feedback helped me to adjust and fine-tune it more times than I care to admit. My goal is to provide you with powerful tools that are only as complex as needed to do their designated job. The structure of the First 100-Day Plan, therefore, contains a few strategic guidelines that contribute to its effectiveness.

The Actions Are Prompts, Not Prescriptions

The high impact actions do not tell leaders *how* to proceed. Instead, they describe at a macro level *what* leaders must do to steer projects toward successful implementation. In this way, the actions function as prompts that provoke your coachees to take contextualized and relevant action within their dynamic and unique organizational context.

For example, using the first action in Phase I, imagine saying something along the lines of this to a leader you coach: *"We know that one of the first things a leader does to give projects a good launch is that they link the benefits of the change initiative to school and district data, and show how the project is coherent with the vision of the organization. Given your project and the culture and context you work within, what do you want and need to do? What does that mean to you? Discuss that while I listen and take notes about your ideas."*

By the way, decisions about specific actions are made by the leaders you coach and not by you. For as professional and experienced as you are as a leadership coach, you do not walk in your coachees' shoes. Instead of giving your opinion about the specific actions your coachees should take, use the action statements as prompts for your coachees. Then, listen to what they say and offer them summaries and paraphrases until they clarify the specific action for themselves.

Timing of Actions

First 100-Day Plans will get the right things flowing, and in a deliberate order that adheres to crucial and vulnerable time periods in the evolution of an initiative. But, they do not impose a strict timeline for completing actions.

For example, some leaders start an action and bring it to fruition within a few days. Other actions may take four to six weeks from initiation to completion. This is especially the case when certain artifacts, deliverables, or decisions are due within a certain time frame. Some actions initiate processes that evolve and mature over the entire first 100 days—even when they begin in Phase I or Phase II. These actions usually render multiple artifacts, deliverables, and events. Still, other actions take more time, need to be revisited or morphed into new actions as the project moves from initiation in the first 100 days to broader and deeper implementation, perhaps for several years. For example, as student achievement data changes, leaders need to revisit the coherence of their project to the needs of their organization.

Processes Leading to Artifacts, Deliverables, Events, Decisions

High impact actions mobilize processes that often produce artifacts, deliverables, events, and decisions. Leaders using the First 100-Day Plan template should include this information in the plan under the column headed, *"Your Specific Actions (include specific people/positions, events, products, deliverables, and decisions)."*

Table 4.1 A Summary of Phases of Action in the First 100 Days

Phase I. The First 33 Days: Build Excitement, Interest, Knowledge, and Demonstrate Systemic Coherence

Actions Prompts	Your Specific Actions (include specific people/positions, events, products, deliverables, decisions)	Start Date and End Date Goal
1. Use data to demonstrate the urgency and relevancy of your project and motivate support.		
2. Articulate how the initiative you want to lead is coherent to the mission, vision, and goals of the organization.		
3. Secure the First Followers.		
4. Assemble a lead team of rapid responders.		
5. Design and roll out professional development for the First Followers.		

Phase II. The Second 33 Days: Metrics, Pilot, Innovate, Tinker, Insight, Communicate

Actions Prompts	Your Specific Actions (include specific people/positions, events, products, deliverables, decisions)	Start Date and End Date Goal
1. Select and articulate to others a few meaningful metrics you will monitor in order to track the impact of your change project.		
2. Refine and continue professional development for the First Followers and extend learning opportunities to others.		
3. Empower the First Followers to get going with the initiative and support them like crazy!		
4. Recognize breakthrough practices and surprising tactics taken by the First Followers that create the greatest gains.		

Actions Prompts	Your Specific Actions (include specific people/positions, events, products, deliverables, decisions)	Start Date and End Date Goal
5. Provide opportunities and forums for you, the First Followers, and the lead team to tell the story about how the project is proceeding.		

Phase III. The Third 33 Days: Celebrate Early Wins and Favorite Mistakes, Revise and Refine, Deepen the Movement, Secure Support, and Remove Barriers

Actions Prompts	Your Specific Actions (include specific people/positions, events, products, deliverables, decisions)	Start Date and End Date Goal
1. Broadcast and celebrate small wins (any movement toward achieving milestones) and favorite mistakes (where you learned the most).		
2. Identify the next wave of participants who can implement and lead the vision, and plan professional development.		
3. Define new goals, identify milestones for the next 12 months, and establish the system for monitoring and reporting indicators.		
4. Gain audiences for yourself and the First Followers, with decision makers and internal and external stakeholders to overcommunicate knowledge and information.		
5. Remove or revise systems, structures, policies, and practices undermining the vision.		

This tool is also available for download at www.WisdomOut.com and www.Corwin.com/Flywheel.

Part III

Practice

The Flywheel
System

chapter 5

An ocean traveler has even more vividly the impression that the ocean is made of waves than that it is made of water.

—Arthur Stanley Eddington, Science Scholar (*The Nature of the Physical World*, 1928, p. 242)

This chapter kicks off our exploration into the actual process of leadership coaching. We begin with an understanding of the entire "system" of leadership coaching.

Systems do stuff. They unify related components that work together to carry out specific activities, processes, routines, and functions. Examples of systems are found everywhere: the respiratory system, the hiring process in an organization, and the plumbing system in your home, to name a few. Users of systems experience its parts as well as the whole, and thereby come to understand its optimal use. People like to think about complex functions as systems because it helps them to see and understand the various components, and to recognize how they influence each other, and ultimately work in concert to do the stuff the system is designed to do.

Flywheel is a system that carries out the process of transformational leadership coaching. Here is the definition of leadership coaching as conceived in this book: *Transformational leadership coaching is an organizational development strategy that supports and sustains meaningful change. Carried out through powerful conversations that lead to action, it is the practice of thought partnering with leaders as they collaborate with others to bring important initiatives to deep implementation, while managing the process of change and deepening the capacity for leadership in themselves, others, and the organization.*

FLYWHEEL LEADERSHIP COACHING COMPONENTS

Figure 5.1 provides you with a visual image of the Flywheel system. When you agree to coach leaders long term, you utilize all components in the illustration (although Component VI is optional). The rest of this chapter provides either a summary of each component in the system, or a reference to the chapter in this book that contains detailed information on the topic.

Figure 5.1 Components of the Flywheel Leadership Coaching System

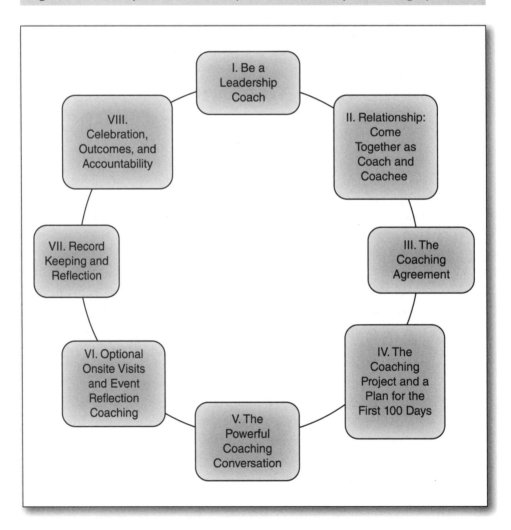

Component I. Be a Leadership Coach

Years ago, I saw a bumper sticker on the back of a car I followed on California Highway 1 from Monterey to Half Moon Bay that declared, "Having a Great Time . . . Wish I was Here!" These words got me thinking about how difficult it is to maintain one's presence in life—how even when the current moment is joyful, our thoughts can turn anxiously to the future, or to nostalgia for the past. Leadership coaches need to acquire heroic abilities to maintain presence when working with their coachees. For leadership coaches, presence means operating in coaching mode, even when their minds threaten to flood with anxiety, judgment, misplaced concern for coachees, and fear of failure.

In the spirit of leadership coaching, the capacity for maintaining your presence is enhanced when values consistent with leadership coaching guide you. From the paradigm of transformational change, at least eight values contribute to your ability to provide great coaching:

Acceptance

Acceptance plays out two ways in leadership coaching. First, it refers to the complete absence of resistance that leadership coaches demonstrate for their coachees and for their coachees' goals. It means coaching with compassion from the coachee's current location in their leadership journey, and toward their eventual destination.

Second, acceptance refers to a coach's ability to see events and data as important information free of labels of "good" or "bad." In this context, acceptance implies a candid and realistic orientation to the world that a leader coaches and then reflects back to their coachees. Doing so encourages coachees to accept events and data with interest instead of resistance. The value of acceptance in this context helps coachees embrace reality, while holding in check the emotional reactions that prevent them from clearly seeing what needs to change (Chodron, 1994).

Humility

When leadership coaches feel certain they know exactly what path their coachees need to take, humility reminds them they are not "The Expert." Humility is a value that reminds you to return to your role as leadership coach: to use your coaching skills, and not impose your will. When you do, you sustain your presence, and your mind does not race ahead to seek answers for your coachees.

Trust

Leaders who coach within the organization where they work must take extra care to create conditions of safety and trust; their colleagues and peers must be able to say anything. They must be able to explore all ideas—even those that are risky and way out of the box—and reflect on successes and perceived failures. This level of trust demands that leaders who coach do not judge or criticize coachees or their ideas. In addition, leaders who coach must keep their opinions and war stories to themselves, believe in their coachees, and stay true and committed to the agenda the coachees set out to accomplish.

It should go without saying that leaders who coach must have a reputation for being trustworthy and maintaining confidentiality, not just when they are in coaching mode, but in all aspects of their leadership work.

Respect

Robb and Kathy Bocchino, cofounders of Heart of Change Associates, a consultant and professional development company, break down the word *respect* into two parts: spect (to see), and re (again). Back in the 1990s, when I had the great opportunity to attend workshops facilitated by the Bocchinos, they said that to respect another person is to see them again as if it were the first time, each time. This definition fits particularly well in the Leadership Coaching model. The value of respect conveys a deep sense of faith in your coachees' abilities to summon the knowledge, skills, and dispositions required in the moment for them to be successful in their work.

Service

Sometimes, Leadership Coaches have deep experience and expertise in the same field as their coachees. This poses a challenge for coaches who find the temptation to coach from their own past and particularly strong perspective. Although coachees may appear relieved when coaches give them advice, this relief is usually short-lived. Advice too frequently comes from the past, and as such is helpful only to the extent that the current situation exactly mirrors the past. In complex and dynamic organizations, this is rarely true.

Equifinality

Equifinality is a principle from open systems theory that allows for the existence of many different pathways to the same outcome (Cummings & Worley, 2005; Weisbord, 1987). Leadership coaches practice equifinality when they follow the pathway taken by their coachees without imposing their own preferred pathway. These leadership coaches respect the self-determination of their coachees, and the meaning that coachees make of the challenges of their lives.

Leadership coaches demonstrate equifinality by asking questions of coachees that stimulate the coachees' unique ideas, dreams, and outcomes. This practice frees coaches to relinquish their past work and life experiences, and to help coachees visualize results that are remarkable for their organization.

Compassion

Boyatzis and McKee (2005) explain that compassion is a manifestation of being in tune with the needs and wants of other people, and then being "motivated to act on our feelings" (p. 77). In other words, compassion is empathy in action. Leadership coaches demonstrate compassion when they use their coaching skills to help others take action toward accomplishing meaningful work. When you consider that every coaching conversation ends with coachees making commitments to take action toward needed and positive change, I believe it is fair to say that coaching itself is an act of compassion.

Mindfulness

In the Zen tradition, mindfulness is sometimes described as feeling the floor under your feet (Shoshanna, 2003). It is the ability to notice thoughts and emotions that come to you when you are coaching, but then return your focus to coaching. Truth be told, most people find it very difficult to completely empty their minds of thoughts. But, when your mind drifts, you can choose to refocus attention on your coachee. During times of stress, when coaches are more likely to respond simply on the basis of old habits and patterns, mindfulness is the antidote to reaction. If you practice mindfulness in your personal life in addition to your coaching relationships, it becomes easier (Landsberg, 2003). You'll know you are becoming more mindful when you feel a reduction in your overall level of stress while coaching.

Component II. Relationship: Come Together as Coach and Coachee

If you accept the premise that leaders are individuals who step forward to start, revitalize, or champion organizational initiatives for positive change, you will have no shortage of coachees. From the superintendent, to the department heads, to the principals, assistant principals, and classroom teachers, multitudes of change leaders are working with passion and care to make a difference. How much better it would be for these leaders if they had a thought partner—a leadership coach like you—who possesses a unique set of skills to support, inspire, and sustain them.

Coach Into an Invitation

Leadership coaches gain coachees through a number of avenues, the most delightful of which is when a leader seeks out the coach and requests coaching. In the world of coaching, we call this "coaching into an invitation."

Unfortunately, in some educational systems leadership coaching is seen as an intervention for poor performers instead of an essential strategy for organizational change and development. I remember one of my earliest coachees who was a successful assistant superintendent in a high-achieving Midwest school district with a hard driving culture that was intolerant of anything less than perfection. "John" wanted a leadership coach to support him as he launched several important initiatives in curriculum and instruction, and simultaneously prepared to make a bid for the position of superintendent when the current superintendent retired. Because long-standing traditions in the district caused people to view leadership coaching as a remediation strategy for leaders who were not up to par, John paid for my coaching out of his own pocket; he did not want the current superintendent or the school board to learn that he was being coached.

The good news is that you are in a position to demonstrate the value of leadership coaching for your organization, or the organizations you serve. And, you are likely to find strong allies, including decision makers in professional development departments who will help to normalize leadership coaching and elevate its status as a preferred model of professional growth. The point is that once you become known as a leadership coach who wants to support colleagues, peers, and direct reports through coaching, savvy leaders seek you out (Chapter 12 presents myriad ideas about how to make leadership coaching an exciting movement in your organization).

Create the Invitation: May I Coach You on That?

Sometimes the invitation to coach is initiated by the leadership coach. In this scenario, you might become aware of a colleague or peer who has taken on an important initiative or complex project, and approach him or her to offer coaching. Perhaps the project leader did not know that coaching was an available option, or like my coachee John, maybe they believed coaching was only for struggling leaders. Whatever reasons might initially prevent leaders from seeking coaching, you can make the first move and extend the opportunity with the words *"May I coach you on that?"* Sure, some leaders will turn you down, but others will welcome your support and accept your invitation, resulting again in the coveted "coaching into an invitation."

Ground the Relationship: The First Meeting

Successful long-term coaching relationships begin with clarity about the focus of coaching and the responsibilities of both the coach and the coachee. From the moment a leader contacts a coach, the tone for their relationship begins to form.

Before leaders agree to coaching, coaches must be prepared to provide direct and clear answers to questions on the minds of coachees. This usually happens during the first meeting between coach and coachee and is guided by an agenda that includes discussion of what the leader wants to be coached on, and agreements about how the coaching will work. The first meeting usually takes about two hours, and may in fact require the leader to do a little homework on their First 100-Day Plan (see Chapter 4). Here is a list of agenda items that structure the first meeting and get important information out in the open:

1. Introductions. Especially important if you are an external coach, or if you do not know the leader very well. Introductions include sharing information about careers, professional experiences, and background, family, and hobbies.

2. The backstory: This is where coachees tell the story about what brings them to coaching.

3. An overview of the Flywheel system and details about how the Powerful Coaching Conversation Protocol works.

4. Logistical details and procedures, such as dates, locations, times of coaching sessions, and methods for meeting (in person, by telephone, or SKYPE—a software program allowing free telephone calls over the Internet).

5. Confidentiality and the coaching agreement (see more details in the next section).

6. Identification of the coaching project (see Chapter 3 for tools), and the first working draft of the First 100-Day Plan (see Chapter 4 for tools to do this).

From the initial invitation to coach, and the first meeting where questions are answered and details are described, the relationship between you

QUESTIONS FREQUENTLY ASKED BY COACHEES IN THE FIRST MEETING

- What will we accomplish in the first meeting? Will I need to do anything to follow up?
- What is Leadership Coaching?
- Will you give me advice during coaching sessions?
- How do we get started and when will the coaching sessions begin?
- How do I determine what to ask you to coach me on?
- Are our coaching conversations confidential?
- What process will you use to guide our conversations?
- For how many months will you coach me? How many sessions will we have during that time?
- What is the schedule for our coaching conversations?
- What happens if I miss or have to reschedule a session?
- How does your background make you a good coach for me?
- How can I get the most out of my coaching experience?
- How many people have you coached before and what do you love about being a leadership coach?

and your coachee is chartered. The next two components also go a long way to create the *initial* bond between coaches and coachees. They are Component III, The Coaching Agreement; and Component IV, The Coaching Project and First 100-Day Plan.

Component III. The Coaching Agreement

The coaching agreement is a tool that effectively specifies mutual expectations and processes for long-term coaching. A formal coaching agreement may strike some readers as excessively specific, but when you coach leaders on projects that last three months or more, I find specificity beats ambiguity every time. As Yogi Berra famously suggested "oral contracts aren't worth the paper they're printed on." Effective coaching agreements that reduce ambiguity, but that don't go overboard with hampering details include these elements: a description of the coaching approach and what leadership coaching can and cannot produce, the promises and commitments of both the coach and coachee, the methods through which the pair will communicate and conduct the coaching sessions, the methods by which the pair will evaluate the process, and the impact of coaching and the dates and times for the entire series of coaching conversations. This last point is crucial. If coaching sessions are not on the calendar, harried leaders with the best of intentions are likely to miss appointments.

In essence, the coaching agreement foreshadows the commitment and trust that both parties will enjoy as the coaching begins. There is an example of a coaching agreement at the end of this chapter (see Figure 5.2).

Component IV. The Coaching Project and a Plan for the First 100 Days

Coachees, not coaches, set the focus for transformational leadership coaching. Although they may not use these exact words, leaders who want coaching essentially say to their coach, "I want to lead meaningful change in my organization—will you coach me?" This component of the Flywheel system includes two tools: the project identification process described at length in Chapter 3 and the First 100-Day Template provided in Chapter 4.

As you already know from reading Chapter 4, the First 100-Day Plan is an invaluable tool for focusing each of the Powerful Coaching Conversations. For coachees launching a new initiative or revitalizing an existing initiative, First 100-Day Plans prompt coachees to initiate high impact actions to get their projects moving. Initiatives that survive initiation and implementation and are fully integrated into the organization and culture need to be sustained through a process of renewal where interestingly enough, the high impact actions from the First 100-Day Plan are again useful and relevant.

Component V. The Powerful Coaching Conversation

Once coachees have a working draft of their First 100-Day Plan, the actual coaching gets underway. Long-term coaching occurs through a series of powerful coaching conversations, driven by excellent communication skills packaged for coaching (which are fully explored in Chapters 7, 8, 9, and 10), in a protocol that creates a flexible framework for guiding coachees from uncertainty to action.

At the risk of revealing the extent of my geekiness in leadership coaching, I believe that the Powerful Coaching Conversation is a thing of beauty, and I am not alone in my admiration for the science and art that makes these conversations work. Dr. Tracee Grigsby-Turner, supervisor of professional development in the Alief Texas Independent School District, poetically says, "It is like a meditation. It requires much of the mind even as it nourishes the spirit" (the Powerful Coaching Conversation protocol is found in Chapter 6).

Component VI. Optional Onsite Visits and Event Reflection Coaching

Transformational leadership coaching and the relationship between coaches and coachees deepen tremendously when coaches spend time with leaders during the workday. As an external coach, there is nothing I enjoy more than spending a half or full day shadowing the leaders I coach. Not all of my coaching agreements include onsite days. But when they do, these visits are not haphazard. They are timed to occur on days when my coachees are neck-deep in the work of their projects.

For example, I've been coaching "Elizabeth," a superintendent in a rural district in California for three years now. Just this year, we agreed to include two site visits coinciding with: (a) two significant meetings, (b) school walk-throughs, and (c) presentations to board members related to her project. On these days, we also schedule powerful coaching conversations. During my visit, I take copious notes which I lay out for Elizabeth at the start of our coaching conversations. From these notes, Elizabeth selects the focus of the conversations.

Internal coaches who are colleagues of the leaders they coach can do the same: visit, observe, take notes, and then present the notes to coachees who select the focus of subsequent coaching conversations from them.

Component VII. Record Keeping and Reflection

Because coaching conversations are complex, engendering many ideas that simultaneously compete with each other, leadership coaches have a structured set of note-taking resources to use during coaching sessions. It is vital that coaches have a journal, or some other note-taking tool to capture the coaching conversations as they take place. Note-taking resources not only create a visual memory of commitments and content from each conversation, but also during conversations, they give form to the connections between the coaching process and what it produces for coachees. Note-taking resources also create a historical record of the progression of the projects and goals.

Here are some practical tips for establishing your record-keeping system:

- Create an electronic folder for long-term coaching agreements, with a separate folder inside for each coachee. Within each folder, maintain copies of relevant documents, such as the coaching agreement, First 100-Day Plan, calendar of coaching sessions, copies of e-mails, and the coaching journal.
- Maintain a coaching journal for each coachee. Use the journal to record notes during each conversation. These notes are confidential

and usually destroyed when the coaching agreement ends, or shortly thereafter. Journals hold your private rough notes from each coaching conversation. They document not only what the coachee said, but also your reflections as you focus on what your coachees deem significant.

- Out of your rough notes, create a brief summary or list of "aha!" moments and insights gained by the coachee during the conversation, and e-mail them to the coachee at the end of each conversation. Most importantly, include in this follow-up e-mail any actions the coachee committed to at the end of the conversation, and anything you promised as well (e.g., to send an article, a tool, or a book reference). Be sure to copy yourself on the e-mail memo and save it in the file of the coachee.

- Keep a master calendar of coaching conversations in order to easily add them up, if necessary. This is important if, as part of the coaching agreement, the coachee or another person in the system asked you to provide feedback on the number of coaching conversations you provided.

Component VIII. Celebration, Outcomes, and Accountability

Leaders enter into coaching relationships committed to producing results for themselves and for their organizations. Coaches enter coaching relationships committed to adding value to the leader's work. These two sets of commitments provide an overarching framework for outcomes, celebrations, and accountability.

During the first meeting, both parties clarify what they expect from each other in the form of promises to maintain these commitments. The promises denote accountability to each other and to the coaching process, and they imply accountability to oneself, and to the organization. Coaches with good reputations would never let their coachees down by failing to carry out their coaching responsibilities. At the same time, coachees have a passion for accomplishing something that could make a profound difference in their organization. In the inspiring words of the late Steve Jobs, these leaders and coaches want to "Leave a ping on the universe." By celebrating small and early wins, and by holding oneself accountable for leveraging leadership coaching toward organizational results, coaches and coachees work together to create needed change. Please see Chapter 11 to explore ways to measure the impact coaching has on leaders and organizations.

ADDITIONAL TOOLS RELATED TO THIS CHAPTER

| **Figure 5.2** | Flywheel Leadership Coaching Agreement |

Flywheel Leadership Coaching Agreement (Sample)

This agreement between Leadership Coach _____ and Coachee _____ begins on _____ and ends on _____.

Leadership Coaching, which is not advice, consulting, therapy, or counseling, is designed to support you in achieving a significant leadership project, to create outcomes that invite leadership and learning for you, and benefits for your organization. Your coach does not provide solutions, or tell you what to do.

This agreement for Leadership Coaching lasts for _____ months and consists of _____ coaching conversations per month. Coaching sessions will take place in person/over the telephone/SKYPE/other and will last about 60 minutes. When sessions are conducted by phone or SKYPE, coachees are asked to call their coach at the scheduled times, at this phone number/SKYPE ID: _____ _____.

Throughout the coaching relationship, we will focus conversations on your Leadership Coaching Project.

Promises of the Coach: I promise to . . .	Promises of the Coachee: I promise to . . .
• Preserve confidentiality. • Use the 100-day Leadership Project to focus the coaching relationship. • Use the Powerful Leadership Coaching Conversation process. • Listen, ask clarifying and mediating questions, ask thought leadership questions, and make observations in order to support you in achieving your goals. • Schedule in advance the agreed-on coaching sessions, about one hour each, over the agreed time period. • Ask coachee for feedback about how coaching is working for them. • Care about your project and your personal journey to leadership.	• Identify an important leadership project, write up a plan for the first 100 days, and come prepared to talk about it. • Participate in the *Leadership Coaching Powerful Conversation* process. • Follow through on commitments and take action between each coaching call. • Participate in the scheduled coaching sessions, about one hour each, over the agreed period of time (missed calls are not rescheduled). • Provide my coach with honest feedback about how the coaching is working for me.

Evaluation

• At the end of each conversation, the coachee states whether or not the call was beneficial (Yes or No and anecdotal comments).
• Key indicator data for milestones and outcomes declared in the coaching project.
• Coach records the number of actual coaching conversations. These data are provided to the Coachee and the Coachee's organization as requested, however the content of the conversations is confidential.
• A final interview about the coaching experience is conducted by the coach with the Coachee at the end of the coaching engagement.

Our signatures on this agreement indicate understanding and agreement with the information outlined above.

Signatures and Dates

Coachee: _____ Date: _____

Coach: _____ Date: _____

This tool is also available for download at www.WisdomOut.com and www.Corwin.com/Flywheel.

The Powerful Coaching Conversation

An Overview

chapter 6

> *The most fruitful and natural exercise for our minds is, in my opinion, conversation.*
>
> —Michel de Montaigne (*The Essays: A Selection*, 1580/1994)

Flywheel Leadership Coaching is a system composed of several components. Although each component is crucial to the effectiveness of the Flywheel system, it is Component V, the Powerful Coaching Conversation, which gives the leaders you coach the vivid experience of *being* coached.

Figure 6.1 displays the Powerful Coaching Conversation protocol. I encourage you to use the protocol as a transfer tool or job aid: keep it in front of you while you coach until you internalize the process, and feel comfortable with the associated skills. For a full-color copy of the Powerful Coaching Conversation protocol, please come to www.WisdomOut.com and www.Corwin.com/Flywheel.

A PROCESS ENGINEERED FOR INSPIRATION

According to the 2009 International Coach Federation Global Coaching Client Study, effectiveness of the coaching process is one of the top attributes that coachees look for in their coaches. Coachees depend on coaches to bring a coaching methodology to the partnership that allows them to accomplish their goals. In other words, coaches must have a well-articulated conversation process, and must confidently and adaptively use it.

Figure 6.1   The Powerful Coaching Conversation Process

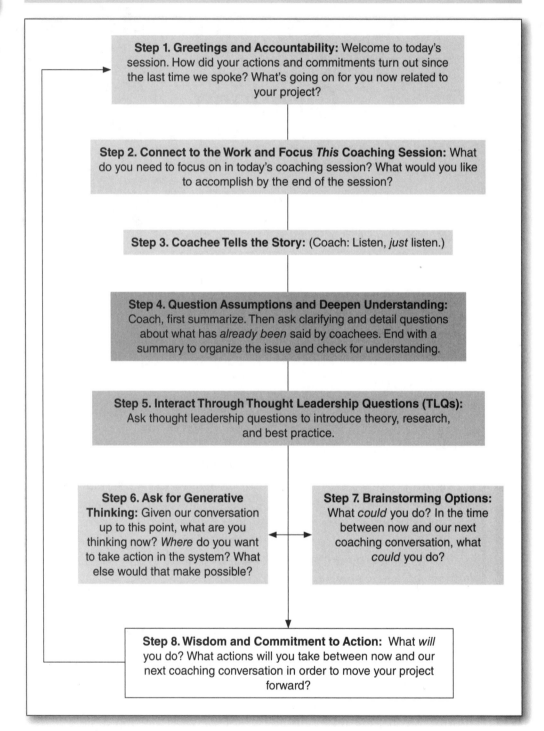

This tool is also available in full color for download at www.WisdomOut.com and www.Corwin.com/Flywheel.

The Powerful Coaching Conversation used in Flywheel is specifically engineered to lead coachees from a current reality, where the next steps of their project are unclear or undefined, to a new reality where the next steps are clear, and they feel confident taking them. This is not to suggest that the leaders you coach feel confused about what to do in every coaching session. Sometimes, they simply have not had one reflective moment during their demanding day to sit down and fully think things through. Whether or not coachees feel stress about knowing the actions that will best move their project forward, if they have the opportunity while in the company of a skilled and compassionate coach to hear and understand their own thoughts, it provides an oasis in a hectic day.

HOW THE POWERFUL COACHING CONVERSATION PROCESS WORKS

The Powerful Coaching Conversation protocol is a guide for full-length coaching conversations. The order of the steps presented in the Powerful Coaching Conversation Protocol is not accidental. They are engineered to create a conversational flow where the coach matches the coachee's developing thought process with communication approaches that engender empowerment and action. Coaches who rush the early steps in the protocol in order to get to the action steps at the end of the protocol diminish the power of coaching and nearly always guarantee frustration for coachees who end up feeling rushed and manipulated.

The Powerful Coaching Conversation Process is not a script. And, in spite of its presentation as a flow chart starting at the top of the page and ending at the bottom, it is not meant to impose a rigid and linear exchange. Instead, the flow defines a dynamic process within space and time parsed over 30 to 60 minutes, where the conversation adapts and readapts as coach and coachee traverse the ground in between uncertainty and wisdom.

The Meaning of the Colors

Every step in the Powerful Coaching Conversation is represented by a color imbued with meaning that conveys information beyond the words found on the page. As you coach, the colors are meant to trigger within your mind the essential principals of transformational leadership, and transformational change (go back to Chapter 1 for a review). Here is an index to the colors:

- Steps 1 through 3. In nature, light green represents life and the potential for growth. Within the protocol, light green represents the wisdom potential that exists inside every single person, even when they are steeped in self-doubt. The first three steps of the protocol are displayed in light green to remind you that the purpose of coaching conversations is to bring out the wisdom of coachees. This begins with listening. Just notice at this point that green appears again, but in a deeper shade in Steps 6 and 7 of the protocol.

- The color brown represents the earth. It evokes feelings of being grounded and of acquiring steadiness. It also suggests the process of "unearthing" assumptions. The color brown is seen in Step 4 where coaches offer summaries and ask detail and clarification questions about what the coachee has brought up so far in the coaching conversation. These questions help coachees uncover assumptions and allow them to view their beliefs with a fresh perspective.
- The color blue represents the vastness of the sky and conjures feelings of leadership and innovation. Blue appears on Step 5 in the protocol where the Thought Leadership Questions (TLQs) are introduced. TLQs lift coachees beyond what they know, and they expand the mind to new possibilities. In Step 5, coachees often acquire insights that challenge the assumptions they unearthed in Step 4.
- The dark green you see in Step 6 and Step 7 acknowledges that through the conversation, coachees have accessed deeper levels of wisdom. In Steps 6 and 7, coachees use the insights gained in Step 5 to recognize systemic possibilities, and to brainstorm potential actions.
- White surrounded by dark green in Step 8 represents enlightenment that translates into commitments to wise action.

When you internalize the Powerful Coaching Conversation Protocol, the colors will become a shorthand trigger for the purpose of each step in the conversation. In the next section, we focus on each step within the protocol.

STEP 1. GREETINGS AND ACCOUNTABILITY

Step 1 (light green): *Greetings and Accountability* provides space for coaches and coachees to welcome each other to the current conversation and for the coachee to update the coach on events related to their leadership work that transpired between the last coaching conversation and now. Greetings reignite the rapport between you and your coachees; this rapport grows and deepens with each new interaction. At the same time, the focus on accountability early in the coaching conversation conveys the message that while leadership coaching is personal and compassionate, it is a strategy for leadership development and organizational change.

Accountability for Actions

After you welcome your coachees to the current conversation, summarize the commitments they made at the end of the previous session and invite them to talk about what happened in the system as a result of those actions. Your invitation sounds something like this: *"At the end of our last coaching session, you made two commitments to action. First, you made a commitment to meet with your teammates to describe the writing rubric and to ask if anyone would be interested in trying it out. At that meeting, you also wanted to show your colleagues how you used the rubric with students the previous week. Second, you made a commitment to watch the webinar provided by the state department on writing rubrics because you wanted to learn how to align the rubric you use with the rubric they use. How did those two actions go? Tell me all about it. Bring me up to speed."*

What Coaches Do In Step 1

In Step 1, coaches essentially ask just two questions: how are you and how did your commitments to action turn out? These two questions initiate the coachee's narrative. The rest of the time, coaches listen and take notes. As coachees speak, coaches listen and resist interrupting the flow of the story with questions and comments. Instead, coaches take notes and notice where the project seems to be moving forward, where the snags appear, and what their coachees think and feel about the whole thing.

A Need for Restraint

During Step 1, and certainly throughout the entire coaching conversation, coaches should refrain from asking questions out of personal curiosity or "need to know." But, they also need to restrain themselves from asking a lot of questions or making comments about anything the coachee says. The reason for restraint at this point of the conversation is this: until Step 2, when the

---

STEP 1 SUMMARY

What Coaches Do

- Greet coachees and invite them to tell the story about how the actions from the last coaching conversation turned out.
- Take notes and convey sincere interest and care.
- Refrain from asking questions or making comments that interrupt the flow of the narrative.
- Notice consequential references to the overall goals of the coachee.

What Coachees Do

- Summarize the story about how the actions from the last coaching conversation turned out.

Results of Step 1

- A reflective narrative from the coachee about what happened in the system when they took action to move their project forward.

coachee defines the focus of *this* coaching session, the relevant pieces from the narrative in the first step cannot be known. Coaches who interrupt the coachees' story with irrelevant questions derail the flow and often cause the coachee to lose his or her train of thought. Coaches need to relax, listen, and write so that they can *receive* the story the coachee has to tell. Later, in Step 4 coaches *do* ask questions and seek to clarify and understand the narrative. But, by Step 4, coaches understand so much more about what matters to the coachee and therefore ask better, and more helpful questions about relevant and urgent parts of the story.

Closure and Transition to Step 2

When coachees complete the narrative about how their actions went and what happened, coaches summarize the status of the project, as related by the coachees. The coach says something like this: *"Thanks for that update. To summarize, and tell me if I have this right, the meeting with your team went pretty well, with the exception of one colleague who balked at the amount of work it might take to put the rubric together. You also watched the webinar from the state department and gained at least three good ideas about how to proceed with your rubric design."* The summary statement coaches make at the end of Step 1 signals movement into Step 2, which invites the coachee to declare the focus of *this* conversation.

STEP 2. CONNECT TO THE WORK AND FOCUS *THIS* COACHING SESSION

In Step 1, we see coachees updating coaches on what has transpired over the *past* week or two between coaching sessions. Conversely, Step 2 thrusts the coach and coachee back into the *present* moment, and asks coachees to identify the focus and desired goals of *this* session. Step 2 acknowledges the events that took place in the lives of coachees between coaching sessions, but more to the point, it focuses today's conversation *in light of* events that transpired since the last conversation. In other words, events in the system since the last conversation provide the context for the focus of the current conversation. Coaches initiate the work of Step 2 by saying something like this: *"Now that you've brought me up to speed, and as it relates to this work, what do you want to focus on in today's coaching conversation?"*

Sources of Focus

The focus selected by coachees in Step 2 comes from two compelling sources: either the First 100-Day Plan, or from antagonistic forces, windfalls, and opportunities—the neither unusual nor rare turn of events that occur in complex organizations, for better or worse, and in spite of all the best laid plans. When the actions taken by your coachee create unexpected results that derail important work, leaders often want to focus their coaching conversations on figuring things out.

Antagonistic Forces, and Windfalls, and Opportunities

On occasion, coachees find themselves facing leadership adversities and forces of resistance or politics that zap their energy. In these circumstances, coaching sessions can focus on supporting the coachee's resolve to stand strong against these adversities so that they can refocus and reenergize for their project. Similarly, when actions create unexpected opportunities and windfalls, coaching sessions can focus on leveraging them for more success.

Establishing the focus of each coaching conversation is crucial to your work as a leadership coach. In fact, it structures the rest of the entire conversation. What your coachees identify as the focus for the conversation trains your coaching mind onto relevant information that comes up in the conversation from this point forward. The focus allows you to make sense of what you hear, and place it in the context of what your coachees want to achieve.

Before moving on to Step 3, coaches repeat the declared focus of this conversation back to the coachee and remind him or her that the rest of the coaching conversation seeks to illuminate it.

STEP 3. COACHEE TELLS THE STORY

After coachees express the desired goal of the current coaching conversation, coaches invite them to talk about it saying something like: *"So the focus you've selected for this conversation is how to revise the writing rubric and recruit a few team members*

STEP 2 SUMMARY

What Coaches Do

- Ask coachees to identify the focus and goals of *this* coaching session.
- Refer to the First 100-Day Plan, or other plans as sources for focus, or to other events that transpired around this work between coaching sessions.

What Coachees Do

- Identify what they want as the focus of this coaching conversation, in light of the larger project and the events that transpired after the last conversation.

Results of Step 2

- The focus for the current conversation in light of the narrative told in Step 1.
- A framework for what you will listen for as the conversation progresses.

to use it. You also said you wanted to find ways to persuade your reluctant colleague to see that ultimately the rubric will save time and not create more work. Tell me all about that."

The Value of Listening

Once you invite your coachees to talk, the only thing you can do is listen. *Just listen.* In Step 3, listening is the primary tool used by the coach. In fact, it is not overestimating its importance to say that listening is *the* most important tool of every great coach (Chapter 7 is entirely devoted to the topic of listening).

The type of listening required in leadership coaching is listening with nothing added, nothing altered, nothing resisted, and nothing judged (Nichols, 1995). To listen this way is to listen from a rock solid foundation that disallows terrible communication habits, such as interrupting, taking over the story, and inserting comments about what you think and feel. None of these habits are productive in a coaching relationship, and they are not very helpful in other relationships, either (Goulston, 2010; Nichols, 1995).

STEP 3 SUMMARY

What Coaches Do

- Summarize the focus identified in Step 2 and invite coachee to talk about it.
- Listen. Just listen. Be especially tuned in to information that serves the coachees' focus and what they want to accomplish long term.
- Take notes and use body language to convey listening and care.

What Coachees Do

- Say everything that comes to mind about the focus without coming to conclusions just yet about actions to take.

Results of Step 3

- A narrative about what coachees know about, think about, and feel about the focus area.

What Coaches Do in Step 3

Aside from taking notes and using body language (smiles, head nods, eye contact, leaning forward) to convey engagement and care, during Step 3 coaches listen. They *just* listen. Coaches who deprive themselves of listening to their coachees in Step 3 of the coaching conversation do themselves a grave disservice. When it comes time for coaches who have not been listening well to speak and ask important questions (as they are called to do in Steps 4 and 5), they have only their own thoughts, opinions, and experiences to draw on.

Coaches who do not listen well lack the crucial and relevant information that can come only from their coachees, to form the things to say, and the questions to ask. If you do not listen well in Step 3, you can only speak from your point of view—not in service of your coachees.

STEP 4. QUESTION ASSUMPTIONS AND DEEPEN UNDERSTANDING

In Step 4, coachees uncover assumptions that have been supporting and justifying unquestioned (and often unhelpful) beliefs and inclinations. Coaches facilitate these understandings by asking detail and clarification questions (see Chapter 8) about what appear to be the most important aspects of the coachee's narrative.

Coaches transition the conversation from Step 3 to Step 4 by summarizing what coachees said in Step 3. It sounds something like this: *"Beth, in a minute I'm going to ask you some clarifying and detail questions. But, first I'd like to summarize what you've said so far about the writing rubric and how to persuade your peers to give it a try. It sounds like you have three main priorities for the rubric itself—making it user-friendly, keeping it rigorous, and aligning it to subsume the qualities the state department expects. You also said you see two challenges—persuading at least three colleagues to use it in addition to the usual writing assessment approaches, and making sure that before they agree to use it, the one recalcitrant colleague does not sour the others on the idea. Do I have that right?"*

Once coachees agree with your summary, go ahead and ask clarifying and detail questions about what they brought up in the conversation, and

---

STEP 4 SUMMARY

What Coaches Do

- Begin with a summary of the narrative from Step 3.
- Ask clarifying and detail questions about information brought up by coachees that is relevant to the focus of this conversation, and the overall goals of the coachee's project.
- Summarize and paraphrase responses as needed.
- Take notes and use body language to convey listening and care.

What Coachees Do

- Engage with the coach in response to the questions asked.

Results of Step 4

- Deeper understanding of the focus area and the context and culture surrounding the coachee and the project.
- Revelations about assumptions and beliefs.

continue to offer summaries and paraphrases about the most important aspects and essence of the unfolding story. In Chapter 8, you also learn how to use a tool called "The Ladder of Inference," which is very helpful when you ask detail and clarification questions.

From this starting point, the coaching conversation moves on to Step 5, and the introduction of Thought Leadership Questions.

STEP 5. INTERACT THROUGH THOUGHT LEADERSHIP QUESTIONS (TLQS)

Step 5 begins when coaches and coachees feel complete with the work of Step 4. Coaches introduce this step by saying something to the effect of, *"Well Beth, now that we both have a good understanding of what's going on for you, let me ask you a series of Thought Leadership Questions that allow you to further illuminate your thinking, and that might engender helpful insights."* Of course, you don't have to use these exact words. The point is that the questions you ask in Step 5 of the coaching conversation inject new ideas into the conversation—this is why I call them "thought leadership questions" (Chapter 9 is dedicated to TLQs, and additional examples are also in the Appendix).

In short, what distinguishes Step 4 from Step 5 is this: In Step 4, coaches ask questions in order to promote a deep understanding of what the coachee has *brought up so far*. In Step 5, coaches ask TLQs to provoke new ideas and new possibilities, and in effect to promote understanding of what has *not yet been addressed* by coachees, but that are still relevant to the conversation.

Thought Leadership

In Step 5, coaches ask coachees to think bigger,

STEP 5 SUMMARY

What Coaches Do

- Ask TLQs in order to provoke thinking, and to put forth the best of what is known about what the coachee wants to accomplish.
- Refrain from giving advice, opinions, or telling the coachee what to do.
- Avoid pushing coachees for solutions (see Steps 6 and 7), just allow them to explore ideas.

What Coachees Do

- Engage with the coach in response to the questions asked. Be willing to say everything that comes up about the topics introduced through the questions.

Results of Step 5

- A new narrative that contains insights, ideas, and possibilities that extend and deepen what the coachee knows or thought possible.
- Creates a desire to learn and know more.

broader, and beyond what they currently understand, are aware of, feel, or believe. Through the skillful application of TLQs, leadership coaches put relevant ideas and theories on the table where their coachees can ponder them. TLQs help coachees expand and shift their perspective. As they work with the TLQs, your coachees begin to experience breakthrough insights, what Costa and Garmston call "cognitive shifts" (1994). They may suddenly understand what is missing in their vision, what is important, and they come to understand events within a systemic context.

Step 5 of the coaching conversation begins to wind down when coachees express new insights and reflect on how they can shift the current reality described in Step 3. Sometimes, during the course of responding to the presented TLQs, your coachees uncover a more relevant, nuanced reality, and they revise their narrative from Step 3. As coachees settle into these new understandings, they pause a bit longer and sometimes express amazement at what they now understand. They might say something like, "Hmm. It is quite interesting to see how I now view my situation!" Statements like this clue coaches to move the coaching conversation on to the next steps, which sometimes happens fast and furiously, especially when coachees experience exciting and engaging breakthrough thoughts.

STEP 6 AND STEP 7. GENERATIVE REFLECTION AND BRAINSTORMING

Step 6 begins with coachees recognizing where the system offers the best chance for action. This is akin to finding a strategy—an approach or a way into an existing reality in order to mobilize change. Step 7 goes hand in hand with Step 6 because it asks coachees to brainstorm the possible actions the coachee could take, once they begin their approach.

A Different Place

What I love most about Steps 6 and 7 is that these steps acknowledge that your coachees have changed. As the dark green color intimates, through the process of the Powerful Coaching Conversation, coachees have uncovered a deeper level of wisdom within themselves. Steps 6 and 7 invite coachees to leverage the stunning insights derived from Step 5 into action to move their project forward. During brainstorming, coachees can also take risks and explore the best and worst of what could happen in the real workplace.

While facilitating Steps 6 and 7, you return to using the great coaching skills you have employed thus far: listening, asking for details or clarification as needed, and summarizing and paraphrasing what seem to be the important

---

STEPS 6 AND 7 SUMMARY

What Coaches Do

- Acknowledge that coachees are thinking differently and see new possibilities as a result of the coaching process so far.
- Invite coachees to describe where they think action is possible and brainstorm ways to move forward.

What Coachees Do

- Identify where action is possible, given the context and culture of the system they work within, and brainstorm ways to move forward.

Results of Steps 6 and 7

- Clarity on the possibilities for action.

---

ideas. The communication for Steps 6 and 7 might sound something like this: *"Beth, given our conversation up to this point, including all of the great insights you had in response to the TLQs I asked you, what are you thinking now? Where do you think you could take action? What are the possible actions?"*

STEP 8. WISDOM AND COMMITMENT TO ACTION

As the coaching conversation proceeds toward conclusion, coaches move to Step 8. Step 8 is exciting because coachees usually feel an incredible sense of wonder at the insights they had during the coaching conversation. By this point in the coaching conversation, and if coaches have skillfully and mindfully activated the tools along the way, coachees have clarity about the next actions to take that will move their project forward, and are eager to get started. They feel enlightened, light of step, and self-empowered to reenter the complex demands of their organization, and to take inspired action in order to make good things happen.

Coaches segue the conversation from Steps 6 and 7 to Step 8 by saying something along the lines of, *"Well, we are at the end of our time together, and you've identified several actions you could take now. What actions will you commit to take between now and our next conversation?"* Coaches support coachees in committing to one to three actions. These actions often involve other people, but they are actions coachees can initiate to influence the system they work within.

STEP 8 SUMMARY

What Coaches Do

- Ask coachees to commit to 1 to 3 actions.

What Coachees Do

- Commit to 1 to 3 specific actions that move the project forward.

Results of Step 8

- Knowledge of the focused action that the coachee will initiate between now and the next coaching session.

DRAWING THE CONVERSATION TO CLOSURE

Coaches take the final moment of the conversation to summarize the one to three actions committed to by the coachee and to ask for feedback about the coaching session itself. They might ask, *"How did this session work for you? Is there anything more that I could do for you as your coach?"* In addition, coaches mention the date and time of the next coaching conversation, and make sure that the coachee has the same date and time written on their calendar.

At the end of the coaching conversation, coaches do not add to the list of actions that the coachee has chosen. If the coach gives "homework," it is usually something to read or reflect on that relates directly to the actions the coachee wishes to take, or to leadership challenges that arose during the course of the conversation (to view a video of a complete coaching session, please visit www.WisdomOut.com).

"YOU'RE GOING TO BE GREAT"

When your coachees' actions do not unfold according to their best laid plans, you cannot prevent them from experiencing pain. But, you *can* choose to provide great coaching that helps them find value in each success and each challenge. In the final moments of the Powerful Coaching Conversation, your role is to resonate positive energy and convey belief in the abilities and gifts of your coachees. I end each coaching conversation with this declaration: "You're going to be great." And then I watch or listen for the coachee to start what I call "The Jaunty Walk" (you'll read more about the Jaunty Walk in Chapter 10), as they reenter their world with confidence and a sense of renewal.

Now that we've dissected each step in the Powerful Coaching Conversation, let's consider what becomes possible when the leaders you coach agree to a long-term coaching relationship where they participate in a series of coaching conversations.

A SERIES OF POWERFUL CONVERSATIONS LEADING TO WISDOM AND TRANSFORMATIONAL CHANGE

When the Powerful Coaching Conversation Protocol is used in a series of conversations, every ten days for a minimum of three months, in conjunction with a First 100-Day Plan, then the benefits compound. Likely, your coachees' projects have gained momentum and your coachees have tested their leadership mettle against any number of challenges.

Figure 6.2 graphically represents the compounded effect when leaders enjoy a series of Powerful Coaching Conversations. What do you notice about this display?

Figure 6.2   A Series of Powerful Coaching Conversations

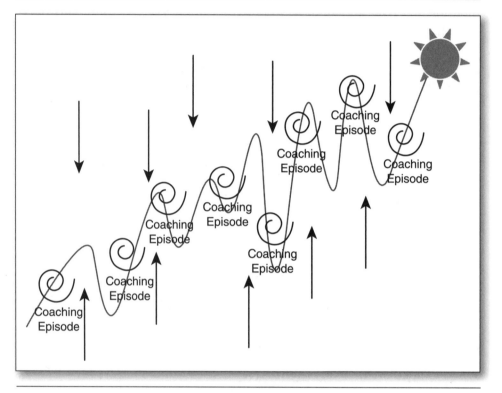

Source: © 2012 Elle Allison-Napolitano and Wisdom Out

A Journey That Trends Up

Most likely the first thing you notice about the series of coaching conversations is that the line, in spite of its peaks and valleys, most certainly trends up and leads to successful meaningful change. You might also notice that the coaching episodes peppering the peaks and valleys of the upward trending line are represented by spirals that also trend up.

Hills and Valleys

I think of leaders on the path to accomplishing meaningful change as the protagonists of a really great story. These leaders are on a quest to make a difference, to solve vexing problems, to ignite leadership in others, and to leave a "ping" on the universe. But, to make a really great story, every protagonist needs an antagonist or two—circumstances and people to block their way and thrust them back into problem-solving mode. Protagonists also need a little help from the people and systems around them to move forward toward their goals. The peaks and valleys represent the ups and downs created by the blessings and banes (represented by the arrows) that come with change work. Coaching is a way to sustain intrepid leaders who ask nothing less of themselves than to contribute passionately to the mission of their organizations.

A Series of Coaching Episodes

As represented by the spirals on Figure 6.2, the coaching episodes peppered on the peaks and valleys of the line provide interludes of thinking and planning as the project unfolds. The Powerful Coaching Conversation takes place within each one of these episodes.

From reading earlier parts of this chapter, you know now that each Powerful Coaching Conversation begins with accountability for prior commitments and ends with commitments to new actions. Notice that the spirals also go from low points to high points. This orientation is meant to convey the idea that each coaching conversation is a microcosm of the bigger picture; each conversation trends upward from ambiguity, confusion, uncertainty, or complacency at the start of the conversation to commitment and empowered action by the time the conversation draws to closure.

Meanwhile, Back in the Real World . . .

The open spaces between each coaching episode on the line represent the space and time back in the "real world" where coachees carry out their commitments and actions. It is in the real world—the nitty-gritty complexity of the organizations these leaders work within—that the story of the change process develops and ultimately where every victory and every challenge takes place. Therefore, it is no mistake that coaching episodes sometimes occur in the peaks and sometimes in the valleys. You see, coaching is not just for the times when trouble brews. In fact, coaching is just as powerful when coachees have traction in their projects, when small wins reveal what elements are working and why (Kahane, 2004).

Each coaching episode is a professional interaction between two people, both of whom care deeply about the topic at hand. Both parties understand that quality coaching has a profound impact on producing outcomes that contribute to the mission of the coachee's school, district, or organization (Joyce & Showers, 1995); therefore, both parties treat the conversation as if it matters. They schedule the coaching episodes well in advance and treat them with the same regard given to other critical meetings or professional development opportunities.

IT AIN'T ALWAYS PRETTY, BUT YOU'RE GOING TO BE GREAT

This chapter is filled with statements that exemplify the essence of what coaches say to coachees during each phase of the Powerful Coaching Conversation. Trust me, the conversations you and I actually hold with coachees ain't so pretty. Coachees will birdwalk, give examples, ask you questions, hyperlink on related ideas, and cover a lot more territory in each phase of the conversation than you might think humanly possible. This is normal, and in fact seems to be essential to the quality of the conversation and the inspired thought that eventually emerges. It is as if everything must first deconstruct and dissolve before coachees can assemble the insights into organized thought and imperatives for action.

In a short period of time, those who want to add coaching to their toolkit can learn to hold these powerful conversations. With practice, coaches internalize the protocol and use it to guide every coaching conversation. Whether coach or coachee, my best advice to you is this: trust the process and trust yourself. You're going to be great.

The coaching conversation process is a dynamic yet structured framework that draws coachees toward efficacy and confidence. Its elegant design creates space and time for crucial coaching strategies to activate. In the next three chapters, we shine a light on the imperative communication skills coaches use: listening, deepening understanding, and asking TLQs.

ADDITIONAL TOOLS RELATED TO THIS CHAPTER

The majority of Powerful Leadership Coaching Conversations take anywhere between 30 to 75 minutes. I find that a coaching conversation that goes beyond 75 minutes starts to become counterproductive—possibly deteriorating into venting, admiring the problem, and procrastination about commitment to actions. Table 6.1 depicts suggested pacing guides when working with periods of 30, 50, and 75 minutes. Bear in mind that the suggested times are exactly that: suggestions. With experience, coaches detect the unique rhythm of each coachee and in the service of their coachees, they become skilled in pacing each coaching conversation.

Table 6.1 Pacing Guide for the Powerful Coaching Conversation

Phase in the Coaching Conversation	If You Have 30 Minutes	If You Have 50 Minutes	If You Have 75 Minutes
Step 1: Greeting and Accountability	About 3 minutes	About 5 minutes	About 10 minutes
Step 2: Connect to the Work and Focus *This* Coaching Session	About 3 minutes	About 3 minutes	About 8 minutes
Step 3: Coachee Tells the Story	About 4 minutes	About 9 minutes	About 12 minutes
Step 4: Question Assumptions and Deepen Understanding	About 6 minutes	About 10 minutes	About 12 minutes
Step 5: Interact Through Thought Leadership Questions (TLQs)	About 6 minutes	About 13 minutes	About 20 minutes
Step 6: Ask for Generative Thinking, and **Step 7:** Brainstorming Options	About 5 minutes	About 6 minutes	About 8 minutes
Step 8: Wisdom and Commitment to Action	About 3 minutes	About 4 minutes	About 5 minutes

This tool is also available for download at www.WisdomOut.com and www.Corwin.com/Flywheel.

Listen, Just Listen

chapter 7

I felt it shelter to speak with you.

—Emily Dickinson *(1878 Letters, 2:599)*

I am in a large presentation room in a hotel in Zambia, speaking carefully to a group of leaders in the ministry of education and at high levels in the university and college system. I am aware that my accent and vocabulary are peculiar to America (and tinged with the occasional sound of Chicago), and may be difficult for my Zambian audience to understand. The topic is Leadership Coaching. Keenly aware of best methods for supporting adult learning, my workshop contains a combination of interactive minipresentations interspersed with exercises that invite leaders to work with each other, apply ideas, and bring the content to life. I have done this sort of work countless times over the past decade or so; rarely do I feel this level of trepidation. I wonder if here in Zambia, do I have the ability to successfully convey the true power of coaching? Or, will I fail to find the right words and lose this opportunity to ignite a passion for coaching in this gathering of key leaders who could use it to transform education in their nation?

The first skill lab in this workshop is called "Listen, just listen." The Zambian leaders in the room gamely listen to the directions. This lab requires partners to take turns as coach, listening as the other talks about a project that matters to them, and that would be good for education in Zambia as well. In the States, I get the occasional eye-roll at this point when at least one person in the audience wonders if this is one of those "touchy-feely" staff development tangents. No one in the Zambian audience looks askance, so I continue. I tell them the exercise will be timed: the "coachee" is to speak for five minutes about their project, and for those five minutes, the designated "coach" must only listen. These are specific directions, and my Zambian colleagues somberly seek clarification. Do you mean we cannot ask a single question? Can't we give encouragement and express our approval? Can't we offer our advice? The answers are yes that is what I mean, and no, and no—for now, don't ask questions, don't give encouragement, or approval, and don't offer advice. Just listen.

These guidelines are so counterintuitive to what people naturally do in a typical conversation that they seem preposterous. Predictably, even people who consider themselves "good listeners" ask questions, interrupt, tell stories, and give advice. I provide the following rules: When in the coachee role, focus on a project that matters to you, speak about it for the entire time (of course, pauses are just fine), and treat it like it matters. When in the coach role, do not interrupt, do not ask questions, do not comment, and treat it like it matters. It is the last set of guidelines, the guidelines for when participants are in the coach role that groans of incredulity can be heard in the room. What? You mean coaches listen for five whole minutes before they get to say a word? Outrageous! How is that coaching?

Yes, I assure my Zambian colleagues, it is true that during this particular five-minute lab coaches listen, just listen. Facing their dubious stares, I promise them that coaches have a chance to talk later in the process. But for now, in this stage of coaching, it is important to listen, just listen. I urge them to trust me and the process as given. They do.

After both partners have the chance to experience the feeling of being listened to and the experience of listening in this remarkable way, we debrief the exercise with the full group. I brace myself and take a breath. Usually the "listen, just listen" exercise evokes strong responses in participants, including the stunning realization that this was the first time in days, months, or even years that someone has listened to them for that long, without interruption, questions, or judging. Usually, participants discover that through listening, coachees actually begin to see their dilemmas more clearly. They begin to feel hopeful. They begin to visualize solutions. I had to wonder, in spite of my American accent and earnest processes whether the power of coaching came through during this simple exercise? To fail at conveying these insights early in the four full-day workshops I am scheduled to lead in Zambia would be disastrous.

At the end of the five minutes, I ask the group: What did it feel like to listen and to be listened to in this extraordinary way? Responses start to come from all sections of the conference hall. "It felt like for once, I was able to hear myself think." "It felt like if I could keep talking, I would figure the whole thing out." "It felt like my coach really cared about me and what I was facing." "I realized that what I first thought was the issue really wasn't it at all." "I heard myself explain the problem I'm facing with greater clarity." "It felt like someone trusted me to know what to do." "It felt funny, but knowing I wasn't going to be interrupted, I was able to be more thoughtful about what I said."

I take a breath, sigh, and smile, happy and relieved to know that my Chicago-American accent and associated vocabulary did not undermine this crucial first exercise—the exercise that universally begins to reveal the power of coaching. Sure, we had just scratched the surface, but what was already becoming clear to the leaders in the room is that this thing called "leadership coaching" could change the way people support, encourage, and inspire the best work of individuals and organizations.

WHAT LISTENING MEANS TO COACHING

The process of "Leadership Coaching" is complex and nuanced—it is a science and an art requiring both technical skill and intuition. Given its demands, many novice coaches are astonished to learn that listening is at the foundation of every great coaching conversation. But, listening is not just a respectful and polite requirement of the conversations you have with coachees; in fact, it is the kingpin—the big daddy skill of coaching. Without listening, leadership coaching does not turn out well at all (visit www .WisdomOut.com and click on the YouTube link to view an entertaining video on listening, featuring my dog).

What Listening Means to the Leaders You Coach

When you *listen, just listen* in the unique way called for in Step 3 of the Powerful Coaching Conversation, your coachees actually begin to see new realities, and some even begin to see solutions. In fact, listening is so important to coaching that the treasured outcomes of coaching—empowerment, inspiration, thought leadership, confidence, and commitment to action—begin to form long before coaches ever say a word.

You see, "coaching" does not occur in the coach's speaking (Hargrove, 2007), but in the interludes created by the coach's attentive silence. Just as in the training in Zambia, invariably when I ask participants in my leadership coaching workshops to raise their hands if they had a new insight about the issue they discussed while their partner coach was just listening, hands shoot up throughout the room. At this point, I enjoy announcing with dramatic flair and flourish, "Ladies and gentlemen . . . welcome to coaching!"

Love and Shelter

When we listen, we show that we care. Some people even say that listening is a form of love (Apatow, 1998). When the people in your life, including the colleagues and peers you coach have the clear impression that you are listening to them, they assign all kinds of meaning to it. For some, they believe listening means that you value them, and you think their ideas are important. For others, they believe it means that you trust them to know their own minds—that you see them as strong, smart, courageous, empowered, and wise. In contrast, no matter how much you try to fake it, if the people you coach get the impression that you are *not* listening to them, they invariably feel undervalued, unimportant, stupid, silly, unenlightened, and insignificant. Michael Nichols claims in his book, *The Lost Art of Listening*, that when a person is not listened to, it is "hard on the heart" (1995, p. 35).

This mindful approach to listening is what master coach Paul Axtell talks about as treating the conversation and the person as if they matter (2009). People who feel that they and their ideas matter see possibilities where previously none seemed to exist. They also see themselves as capable of much more than they originally believed, and allow themselves to dream.

What Listening Means to the Coach

When coaches listen well, without judgment, resistance, or arrogance then what transpires during the coaching session is relevant and compassionate. Coaches who listen inspire trust in their coachees who feel assured that their coach understands them and their unique situation. Within this trusting relationship, coachees share more details, say more about what they really think and feel, entertain more risks, and wrestle with tougher issues.

Listening is how coaches stay in the present moment, gathering critical data from which to speak. At the start of the conversation, coaches who fail to listen when their coachees declare how they want to focus their attention, and what they want to achieve by the end of the coaching session, deprive themselves of the very information they need to move the coaching session forward. After all, how can a coach ask relevant and thought-provoking questions when they don't understand the issue at hand from the coachee's perspective?

Coaches who do not listen have no choice but to speak from their own experience, their own point of view, their own assumptions, and biases. For example, coaches who interrupt coachees in Step 3 necessarily shortchange the process in Steps 4 and 5, when they should be asking relevant questions to advance the focus and agenda of coachees. How can a coach ask relevant questions about content and topics that they have not heard or understood? Coaches lacking content provided by coachees are more likely to deliver a boring monologue of their own ideas. This is not what coachees expect from coaching; if they wanted information and opinions, they could read a book, or attend a lecture.

WHAT STOPS COACHES FROM LISTENING?

The idea that one has to listen, *just* listen for a little while without interrupting, commenting, or asking questions makes novice coaches squirm. Beginning coaches simply are not accustomed to listening in this unique way, so it feels awkward and even impolite. It is helpful for coaches to understand that many people, if not most, go days and days without anyone in their lives really listening to them. With no one to listen to them, these forlorn individuals are deprived of understanding their own minds—from hearing and "seeing" their own thoughts.

Habits

What can make listening so difficult for coaches is not that they are required to go five minutes without speaking, but that they have to do battle with the comfortable, but unhelpful habits they have developed over the years that prevent them from really listening in the first place.

Habits are comfortable and parting with them can be painful indeed (Dieken, 2009). For example, some coaches find the pauses between the sentences spoken by coachees intolerable; they just have to break the silence and say something, even when they know it derails the coachees' train of thought. Other coaches are unable to quiet the chaos of their own minds. They become distracted with tangential, but irrelevant thoughts that they may even express. Still others fear that the people they lead will think them incompetent unless they interrupt with brilliant thoughts and opinions—after all, they might rationalize, isn't this what I get paid the "big bucks" to do? While trying so hard to be the leader, these coaches forget that developing other leaders *is* their primary responsibility.

Comfortable, but unhelpful habits include the basics: interrupting, giving advice, having opinions (and not being able to resist sharing them), and taking over conversations that remind them of something. Other habits include the need to "be right," multitasking, thinking about other things, and desperately needing to be known for having marvelous ideas.

Habit Triggers

Thoughtful coaches recognize and interrupt the triggers that set their habits into motion. Some of the more powerful triggers that prevent listening include anxiety, the need to "look good," and feeling desperately in need of personal renewal.

Anxiety and Other Emotions

Coaches do not mean to derail coaching conversations by failing to listen. Sometimes, the habits that prevent coaches from listening are triggered by the emotions their coachees express and display. At other times, the issues discussed by coachees hit close to home and remind coaches of something they too have wrestled with in the past. Or, perhaps coaches "see" the answers clearly, and become anxious to "cut to the chase."

Empathy arises from the strong commitment coaches give to the project and to the outcomes sought by their coachees. Naturally, you empathize with your coachees when they face antagonistic forces in themselves and in their organization. However, in order to listen well you must fortify yourself against becoming completely swamped by the emotions of your coachees. The International Coach Federation (ICF) describes this effort as maintaining a coaching presence, characterized by resistance to becoming overpowered and enmeshed by the emotions of their coachees (2008). Great coaches monitor and regulate their emotions during coaching conversations so that they can be present and able to coach when the emotions of their coachees run high.

Fear of Not "Lookin' Good"

Coaches also must resist the ego's need to "look good" at all costs, even at the expense of coachees. The need to look good in the perceived eyes of others is another major trigger of habits that prevent us from listening. Coaches who have an insatiable need to have all the answers and be the "smart one" in the room are likely worried about how they might look to others. Instead of listening, their thoughts are preoccupied with formulating what they will say next, and how it will sound to their coachees.

In Need of Renewal

Coaches are not perfect people with perfect lives; they have families who need them, they become ill, and they suffer from the same plights that face every other human being on the planet. Leadership coaches who are tired, sick, upset, lonely, and depleted by the challenges in their own lives have very little to give to coaching relationships. Unless they take care of themselves and make time for personal renewal, leadership coaches are unable to listen well during coaching sessions—their minds are simply too preoccupied with other matters.

Coaches and other leaders in need of renewal may also be overwhelmed by tasks they either need to complete, or otherwise remove from their "to do" lists. Let's be honest, most people feel edgy and restless when they do not accomplish some of the items on their "to do" list each day. For coaches, the discomfort that arises from the sense of too many incomplete tasks overtakes their minds and makes listening a challenge. For these coaches, crossing items off their "to do" list is a form of renewal, and they need to set at least 30 minutes aside each day to accomplish one or two of them.

As hard as it is to break the habits that prevent people from listening, make no mistake: Listening is the most important tool of great coaches. With practice and awareness, coaches become cognizant of when they are not listening, and they choose to return to reengage and listen.

WHAT COACHES "DO" WHEN THEY LISTEN

Listening within the coaching conversation is a complex proposition. When coaches listen, they do more than hear the words spoken by their coachees; they maneuver their minds into a mode of functioning consistent with understanding.

Fall to Silence

There is a Zen saying, "Do nothing." Undoubtedly, the idea of "doing nothing" is strange and counterintuitive to most people—as strange as listening is in organizational cultures where quick fixes and unfocused action is the norm. In daily conversations, people have strong urges to express themselves. They want to make points, be heard, convince others, and come across as clever and wise. These impulses make listening (really listening) counterintuitive. To "do" nothing, however, one has to overcome reactions and impulses. Instead of reacting, one must become very active, as the word "do" suggests, in the role of listening. In other words, when coaches listen, they mindfully fall to silence.

Early in the coaching conversation, great coaches are deliberate about listening. After greeting the coachee and establishing the focus for the coaching session, a coach may listen for upwards of five or six minutes before saying anything more than "Uh-huh," "I see," or "Tell me more." Some coaches find all of this listening unnerving. They want to rush toward brainstorming solutions to solve the problem. With experience and willingness to trust the process of coaching, coaches discover that answers cannot be forced, but must be uncovered.

Coachees need to hear their own thoughts. Therefore, coaches must learn to fall to silence. Falling to silence is a lot like "doing nothing." To successfully fall to silence, coaches must choose to override impulses to hurry the coaching process toward premature conclusions.

More Than a Step in the Coaching Conversation

Listening to the coachee's current story is not only a specific "step" near the beginning of a coaching conversation, but also an open tool for the entire coaching conversation. This means that *whenever* you ask questions or provide summaries during the coaching session, you must then fall to silence so that the coachee can reflect and respond. When you fall to silence, you give your coachees time and space to work with the ideas that have developed. Coaches who do not fall to silence after speaking often find themselves delivering minilectures on ideas they embed in the questions they ask. This is a way of taking over the coaching conversation to make it about what they want to say rather than what the coachees need to think about in order to move their project forward.

They Release Their Personal Net of Memories

In his groundbreaking book on dialogue (1999), MIT lecturer William Isaacs writes, "To listen is to realize that much of our reaction to others comes from memory; it is stored reaction, not fresh response at all" (p. 92). Isaacs says these memories predispose us to listen from within a net of our own thoughts that we cast over the words we hear. When you remove the net of your own memories and listen to coachees with a fresh mind, you successfully suspend the judgments and resistance that interferes with listening.

In his book titled *Dialogue*, William Isaacs relates "Emerson once joked that ninety-five percent of what goes on in our minds is none of our business" (1999, p. 84). Following Emerson's observation, the first thing coaches do to release their personal net of memories is they notice and then let go of chatter in their minds about what coachees have said. This chatter is loaded with judgments and resistance, things like, "Uh-oh, this coachee doesn't have a clue!" Or, "I don't see why that matters." The ideas that coaches judge and resist are more relevant for them to explore with their own mentor than they are for sharing with coachees.

In fact, the areas that coaches judge and resist arise most often out of their own experiences and their personal net of memories. To express these ideas out loud

---

TRY THIS

Here is a kinesthetic example to help you experience what it feels like to release your personal net of memories.

1. Stand up and reach your fingertips down toward your feet, with the aim of touching your toes.

2. Go as far as you comfortably can without straining your back or hurting yourself. Notice how far you can go.

3. Now come up and shake out your arms and legs. Take a breath and reach down again and try to go further—not by reaching forward—but through releasing your lower back. Once again, note where your fingertips end. Did they go further than they did the last time?

Most people are able to go further when they release their lower back. This is what it feels like to release your personal net of memories. Think of this experience before every coaching session.

is destructive to the professional relationship between coaches and coachees, and to the results sought by coaching.

They Listen in Service of Their Coachees

When listening, coaches also track, distill, prioritize, and intuit the importance in what coachees say during coaching conversations and then filter that information through what coachees say they want to accomplish long term. I call this listening in service of the coachee.

Although coaches do not interrupt coachees with the observations and insights they have while listening, they do track them in the notes they take while the coachee speaks. As they listen and write, coaches continually consider and reconsider the relevance of each statement uttered by their coachees. Some ideas that initially seem important fade with the next sentence. Other ideas sustain their importance and become the content and focus of the rest of the conversation.

In the first lab of the workshops I conduct, many novice coaches confess they are sorely tempted when they should be listening (*just* listening!) to interrupt and ask their coachees questions, only to learn moments later (because I impose the rule of "listen, just listen" with no questions, interruptions, or comments) that what they intended to inquire about either came up naturally, or was eventually deemed insignificant. In either case, they say they are grateful they were forced by the rules of the lab not to waste precious coaching time exploring something that mattered only incidentally to the coachee.

They Listen With a "Coach's Mind"

Effective coaches listen with a coach's mind for what they know could be important from a systemic perspective for their coachees. This means that coaches listen for what coachees say about a whole host of ideas that could have far-reaching effects. For example, statements your coachees make about relationships, resources, the need for learning, leadership opportunities, cultural dynamics, changes in policies and procedures, and opportunities and threats coming down the pike all provide potential content for rich exploration in the remaining steps of the coaching conversation. Thus, while listening, coaches hear the words of their coachees, recognize and release the personal net of memories that cause them to judge and resist what is being said, and simultaneously track and prioritize important ideas in service of their coachees, and what they wish to accomplish in complex systems.

If you did not believe that listening was difficult before, you might now find the mere idea of listening—something you thought was as natural as breathing—quite daunting! But, fear not. With mindfulness and intent, listening in this way is a practice that eventually becomes a way of being.

LISTENING AND LEADERS WHO COACH

It turns out that listening is a leadership skill as much as it is a coaching skill. Dr. Lisa Sanders, author of *Every Patient Tells a Story: Medical Mysteries and the Art of Diagnosis* (2009), tells of two research studies that found doctors allow patients to talk for an average of just 20 seconds before they interrupt. Some only allow three seconds. Moreover, the doctors in the study rarely if ever go back and ask the patient to finish what they were saying. When the doctors and patients are interviewed separately after the conversation, fifty percent of the time they disagree about the purpose of the visit.

Although Sanders writes specifically about the troublesome listening habits of physicians, many leaders in education frankly admit that they are known for giving answers, rendering judgments, and offering (in their most humble opinion) their point of view. With that approach, almost always the person they are speaking to feels pressured or coerced to follow. To some leaders, giving answers *is* leadership. They fail to see the liabilities that come with having all the answers, all the time. In his book, *Leading in a Culture of Change* (2001a), Michael Fullan writes, "Beware of leaders who are always sure of themselves. Effective leaders listen attentively—you can almost hear them listening. Ineffective leaders make up their minds prematurely, and by definition, listen less thereafter" (pp. 123–124).

Leaders who coach their peers and the people they supervise are obliged to be even more rigorous about listening, especially when they are not in "coaching mode." For it is here, in the daily interactions of leadership that reputations are made. Leaders who are not good listeners when they supervise, advise, mentor, or teach the people who report to them will have a harder time stepping into a coaching role, no matter how much they might wish to do so.

RETURN TO LISTENING

Coaches who realize they have not been listening only make matters worse if they fail to fall to silence and listen. If, while you are coaching, you realize you have not been listening, begin to listen now, and now, and now, and now. Just begin again to listen every moment you realize you have not been doing so.

LISTENING IS THE GATEKEEPER TO GREAT COACHING

Listening is a skill that everyone can improve. With practice, listening replaces habits of interrupting, giving advice, expressing opinions, and making conversations about ourselves. Great coaches understand that listening is the primary communication skill in their toolbox and is the gatekeeper to successful coaching conversations.

The next chapter explores three more communication skills used in leadership coaching: Summarizing, and asking questions that clarify or provide details.

Question Assumptions and Deepen Understanding

chapter 8

We need creativity in order to break free from the temporary structures that have been set up by a particular sequence of experience.

—Edward de Bono (*Serious Creativity*, 1992, p. 17)

Up to this point in the Powerful Coaching Conversation process, your coachees have told you two related narratives. The first narrative, which took place in Step 1, brought you up to date on events that occurred between the last coaching session and this one. In the second narrative, which took place in Steps 2 and 3, the coachee told you what they want to focus on in the *current* session and what they currently know, think, and feel about that focus.

In Step 4, you provide summary statements and ask clarifying and detail questions about what seems to be the most important aspect of your coachee's narrative so far, related to the identified focus and the overall project. As the brown color of earth in Figure 6.1 suggests (download a full-color version at www.WisdomOut.com and www.Corwin.com/Flywheel), these communication skills help to ground you and your coachees with facts and details, but they also help to unearth assumptions. The resulting dialogue reveals the current reality as your coachee sees it and produces two outcomes: (1) you better understand your coachee's situations, and (2) your coachees better understand their own minds *about* the situation. During this process, coachees are often astounded to discover the assumptions that underpin their beliefs and inclinations.

TRANSITION FROM STEP 3 TO STEP 4

Recall from the previous chapter that Step 3 of the Powerful Coaching Conversation process requires coaches to listen, just listen with no interruptions or questions. Coaches move coaching sessions on to Step 4 when they see and feel that the coachee is complete with everything they want to say right now about the focus of today's session.

If, when you are coaching your colleagues and peers, you are unsure about whether or not they want to say more, just ask them. Say something like, *"I'd like to move us on to the next step, but first let me ask you, is there anything else you want to say?"* Once coachees assure you that they are complete with what they wish to say, you'll begin Step 4 with a summary. Recall from the example provided in Chapter 7 that a summary sounds something like this: *"Beth, in a minute I'm going to ask you some clarifying and detail questions. But, first I'd like to summarize what you've said so far about the writing rubric and how to persuade your peers to give it a try. It sounds like you have three main priorities for the rubric itself—making it user friendly, keeping it rigorous, and aligning it to subsume the qualities the state department expects. You also said that you see two challenges—persuading at least three colleagues to use it in addition to the usual writing assessment approaches, and making sure the one recalcitrant colleague does not sour the others on the idea before they agree to use it. Do I have that right?"* Notice that the opening summary helps to organize the many topics and ideas relayed to the coach by the coachee (more about summaries later in this chapter).

Once coachees agree with the initial summary provided by the coach at the start of Step 4, coaches are then free to use all of the communication skills available to them in Step 4. They may ask clarifying and detail questions about what the coachee has brought up so far, and they may continue to offer summaries and paraphrases of the most important aspects and essence of the unfolding story, referring back to relevant ideas that came up in the narratives produced in Steps 1 and 3 and even bringing up relevant information from previous coaching conversations.

COMMUNICATION SKILLS USED BY COACHES IN STEP 4

In Step 4 of the coaching conversation, coaches primarily use a set of three communication tools:

- Summarization: Statements that summarize, paraphrase, or translate what coachees said, without changing meaning and intention.
- Clarification Questions: Questions that clarify ambiguous or confusing parts of a coachee's story.

- Detail Questions: Questions that seek relevant details of important topics raised by the coachee.

Summarizing and Paraphrasing Statements

Statements and paraphrases are not the same thing as retelling the story—where you attempt to say *everything* the coachee said. Instead, summaries and paraphrases seek to encapsulate what is *most important* about what the coachee said, and to organize it in a useful and relevant framework (e.g., according to priorities, processes, impact, lists of events, etc.).

The statements made by coaches to summarize and paraphrase the accounts of coachees have multiple functions:

1. They convey to coachees that you have tracked and understood the most important ideas in the story.

2. They function as questions that invite elaboration, clarification, and details. For example, if a coach offers a paraphrase like, *"You said you are drawn to option B for the following reasons . . ."* the coachee is likely to provide additional information either about option B, or about why they are personally drawn to it.

3. They frame the essential dilemmas, options, or viewpoints through the eyes of the coachee. For example, you could summarize an account provided by the coachee by saying, "It appears you have three priorities, A, B, and C, and they each require different resources."

4. What you select to paraphrase and summarize draws the attention of your coachees to those matters. You make coachees aware of what you discern as important, based on the full context of the coachee's situation.

Here are examples of sentence stems that begin the summary and paraphrase statements made by coaches in Step 4 of the coaching conversation.

- So . . .
- In other words . . .
- You're saying that . . .
- There seems to be two issues here . . .
- You're concerned about . . .
- You're seeing . . .

Beyond deepening understanding, summaries and paraphrases exhibit empathy and create a state of rapport. Hearing your voice describe their situation, your coachees feel less alone and more able to see their way through what previously seemed unique or even peculiar.

Questions That Ask for Details and Clarification

Detail and clarification questions are different from Thought Leadership Questions (TLQs) that are used by coaches to prompt innovative thinking and that do not expect an answer, per se (see Chapter 9). When coaches ask detail and clarifying questions in Step 4, they *do* expect to receive information: the amount of time, the frequency of something, a list, a description, a definition, or an example. Sometimes the answers provided by coachees turn out to be knowable facts. These are answers that anyone could know or look up. Other times, the answers provided by coachees are not knowable facts, but are the coachee's best known answer, based on what they assume, and believe at this point in time—which could very well be the same or different from what other people know, assume, and believe.

Here are a few examples of detail and clarification questions. What observations and assumptions can you make about their characteristics?

- You mentioned students choose reading material from what is available in class. What books do students have access to in your classroom?
- With regard to the new reporting system, are parents required to sign off on the report card? Tell me more about the process.
- So, the board asked you for an update on the strategic plan. What date was the final draft promised?
- You mentioned that your students learn a lot more when they collaborate with each other. When you say collaborate, does this mean group projects or does it mean anytime students work together or come up with ideas together?
- You mentioned you believe in giving students frequent feedback. Tell me more about how often you give student feedback in your classes.

My observations and assumptions about the characteristics of detail and clarification questions are:

_____

_____

_____

_____

_____

_____

What Makes Detail and Clarification Questions Powerful

From the examples provided above, you might have noticed or surmised several characteristics that make detail and clarifying questions powerful:

1. They all begin with a statement that references information spoken by the coachee. This is because detail and clarifying questions do not put new ideas on the table (unlike TLQs, see Step 5). They wrestle only with content already brought up by the coachee. They deepen and ensure understanding about what coachees have said or referenced, up to this point. If you think about it, this only makes sense. After all, how can a coachee clarify or provide details on topics he or she has not brought up yet?

2. They are highly contextual, referring directly to the situation of the coachee and the coachee's operating organization. Contextual stems provide strong assurances to the coachee that the coach grasps important nuances of the conversation from a systemic perspective.

3. The questions all deal with relevant content the coach deems important. How do coaches know what is important? They are guided by the overall goals of the leadership project, the focus of the current conversation, and the unique context and culture of the coachee's organization.

4. The questions are worded in order to reduce ambiguity and flesh out concepts that appear important, but incomplete, or are built on assumptions that have not been fully explored.

Examples of Detail Questions

Here are examples of sentence stems that coaches use to begin questions asking for more details:

- Can you give me details about . . . ?
- Say more about . . .
- Do you have specifics about . . . ?
- What are the details of . . . ?

Here are examples of how some of these sentence stems sound when they are added to relevant information already supplied by coachees:

- "Tell me more about the details of the feedback you would like from the team."
- "Say more about the process you are thinking about."

- "Do you have specific details yet about who will be at your presentation and what they want to walk away with?"
- "What categories appear on the rubric you use?"

Examples of Clarifying Questions

Here are examples of sentence stems that begin clarification questions that coaches use:

- Are you saying X or Y?
- Can you clarify this?
- Something you mentioned sounds vague. Can you clarify?
- Can you give an example of this?
- I'm not sure I understand. Can you clarify this point?
- What do you mean when you say . . . ?

Here are examples of how some of these sentence stems sound when they are added to relevant information already supplied by coachees:

- "When you said 'team leader' do you mean team leader for each grade range or team leaders for each subject area?"
- "Could you clarify what you mean when you say 'new teachers'? Are these teachers who are new to teaching or new to your system?"
- "Can you give me an example of what you mean when you say the system itself is resistant to change?"

As coachees hear their own responses to summaries and to detail and clarifying questions, they begin to see, hear, and understand their "take" on the situation, perhaps for the first time. We all feel that we know and understand our own situations. However, when it comes to complex matters what we think we know is often not what we thought—but we don't know it until we hear ourselves describe it out loud to someone who listens in a way that facilitates this awareness.

THE LADDER OF INFERENCE

When coachees talk about their current situation, they cover a lot of territory. They refer to many ideas, shift between topics, bird walk into stories that cause them to lose track of the point, and make vague and incomplete references to a wide assortment of people, processes, and desired outcomes. In response to the information bombarding them, coaches ask detail and clarifying questions that enable them to sort things out, reduce ambiguity, and flesh out important topics mentioned tangentially. But, coaches also ask detail and clarifying questions because they believe their coachees will benefit from hearing themselves elaborate and illuminate what seems to be at the heart of what they desire and seek.

I once saw a bumper sticker that said, "Your head is like a bad neighborhood. Don't go there alone." I find this quote charming for this simple reason; it is *so* true. Left to our own devices, and fueled by our assumptions, we can innocently interpret visible data inaccurately and either make mountains out of molehills, or lemonade out of rotten lemons. Coaches use clarifying questions, detail questions, and provide summaries and paraphrases to mitigate the faulty conclusions that even highly effective leaders draw from time to time when they are left to explore the contents of their minds alone.

Organizational learning guru Chris Argyris (1993) invented a mental model that helps people understand the cognitive activity of their minds whenever they experience anything in the physical world. He calls it the Ladder of Inference because it reveals how the human mind rapidly arrives at decisions about what to do in response to events and data, as if they were climbing up the rungs of a ladder. The Ladder of Inference is a useful mental model for coaches to use to further focus the questions they ask in Step 4 of the Powerful Coaching Conversation.

Understanding the Ladder of Inference

Let's take a look at what makes the Ladder of Inference such a powerful tool in leadership coaching. As can be seen in Figure 8.1, the Ladder of Inference begins at the *lowest rung* with data and experiences that any person can objectively observe. Argyris says to think of this information as what could be recorded with a video and audio camera.

As soon as individuals witness data and experiences, they move up to the *second rung* of the ladder, where long-held assumptions, beliefs, and previous experiences filter and select only certain information—information that usually conforms to beliefs and assumptions. This step is not visible to others or a movie camera; it takes place rapidly and in the mind of the individual.

Still invisible to others, individuals quickly leap from paying attention only to the data selected after filtering, and they jump to the *third rung* where they add meaning to the selected information—again, based on assumptions and beliefs derived from previous experiences.

On the *fourth rung*, individuals make assumptions based on the meaning added. Assumptions are a shorthand way to fill in missing information or information the individual has not clarified, verified, or checked. This is similar to when you say things like, "Well, I didn't actually talk with Joe Blow about this, but I assume he will want to . . ."

On the *fifth rung*, the individual draws conclusions that explain why people are doing certain things or what has motivated certain events. These

Figure 8.1 The Ladder of Inference

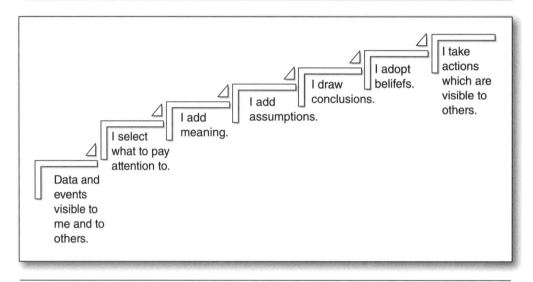

Source: Adapted from Argyris (1993).

conclusions feel like the "truth," and therefore they lead the individual to the *sixth rung* where they adopt these conclusions as beliefs—not just about the current situation, but often about the whole world in general. Especially in the context of leadership, this creates strong negative or positive feelings in the individual who then feels they have to do something.

On the *seventh rung,* out of the beliefs and feelings that came up on the sixth rung, the individual decides they fully understand the situation, and so they take action.

Of course, the actions leaders take are in full view of co-workers and peers in the organization, creating visible information for others to work with (and race up the Ladder of Inference themselves). When the actions of one person based on the data they selected to pay attention to differs from the data that another person selects to pay attention to, both parties scratch their heads in confusion and wonder literally what the heck the other person was thinking. And, as they say in many movie reviews, "mischief ensues."

How Coaches Use the Ladder of Inference

Coaches who reference the Ladder of Inference in Step 4 of the coaching conversation help coachees slow their race up the ladder and challenge assumptions before they take action. Or, if the leader has already taken action based on faulty assumptions, the ladder helps your coachees reflect and take steps to right the course and revise their assumptions. Here are some examples of how you can use the communication tools employed in the Powerful Coaching Conversation and Argyris's Ladder of Inference. Notice the questions are open ended and nonjudgmental, which make the thinking process visible:

- "Tell me more about the data you focused on as you selected the strategies for your school" (*detail question about the data selected on the second rung*).
- "Can you clarify what you mean when you say that the superintendent obviously means to exclude your school from the grant?" (*clarifying question about the meaning added to the data in the mind of the coachee on the third rung*).
- "You said you assumed the committee would want to wait to meet until after the holidays—you've seen that sort of thing before?" (*combination summary statement and detail question about the coachee's assumptions on the fourth rung*).
- "From what you understand about the reluctance of your team members to meet, you feel they need to go back and review what they originally learned about Professional Learning Communities. Tell me more about what should be included in that review" (*detail question on conclusions drawn on the fifth rung*).
- "So, you believe that the data teams value the time provided to meet because they never fail to gather together on Thursday afternoons" (*summary statement about what the coachee believes to be true as determined on the sixth rung*).

The field of organizational learning provides a variety of mental models that are infinitely helpful to coaches. The Ladder of Inference is just one of many, but it is extremely powerful and applicable in Step 4 of the coaching conversation.

THE COACHING CONVERSATION IN STEP 4

Leadership coaching is both a science and an art. As a science, coaches make explicit use of the coaching conversation phases with the knowledge that it will lead their coachees toward understanding and action. For example, in the early phases of the coaching conversation, coachees state what they want to be coached on and what they want to accomplish by the end of the coaching conversation. The focus identified by your coachees alerts you to what to specifically listen for and where to ask questions. As an art, coaches develop a knack for knowing just where within the conversation to linger, clarify, and elaborate so that coachees are likely to have insights about the ideas that are most relevant.

Here is a sample coaching conversation that illustrates a coach artfully using the science of the coaching conversation, asking clarifying and detail questions, and offering summaries and paraphrases:

Coach: "Claire, it's great to be with you for this coaching session. Tell me how the actions you committed to at the end of our last coaching session went and where you are now in your project."

Claire: "Well, as you know I made the decision at the end of our last coaching conversation to meet with the four lead teachers of the core content areas to tell them, for the first time, about my vision to add a process of looking at student work to the Professional Learning Community meetings. I have to say, it went really well considering that this additional process will surely rock a few boats in the teaching ranks when we share it with the rest of the faculty. The lead teachers agreed that this is a necessary step and they also agreed to help me plan the rest of the project. After we talked about it, we decided to ask at least one content area team to try the process and give us feedback on what worked well and where the hiccups occurred. So, I'd like to use this coaching session to think through how to get one teacher team to buy into the idea of using the process for six weeks. I think I also want them to share the experience with the rest of the teachers at faculty meetings along the way. Of course, I'm hoping they will love the new process and that this will persuade other teams to also adopt the process."

Coach: "Claire, let me summarize what I've heard so far. First, the four lead teachers gave you their support, and as a group, you decided that the next step is to recruit a willing team to give the process a try over the next six weeks, provide you and the four lead teachers with feedback, and share their experiences at various faculty meetings along the way." *(summary)*

Claire: "Yes, exactly. I'm really thrilled with the momentum we have at this point. And I think we have a team or two to choose from to pilot the process. I would hate to lose this opportunity to gain early feedback about how the process works in a real team of teachers."

Coach: "Momentum gives you a sense of energy. You sound like you want to strike while the iron is hot, as they say!" *(paraphrase)*

Claire: "I do. See, just one or two teachers have a way of taking the wind out of the sails of every initiative, no matter how much the research supports it. I don't want them convincing the other teachers that the process is a bad one before we even have a chance to see how it works in a real team."

Coach: "Claire, I'd like to ask a clarifying question. When you say you want to pilot the process with a willing team, do you mean a

> team that does not have members who shoot down initiatives no matter what they are?" *(clarifying question)*

Claire: "Yes, that is definitely part of what I'm looking for, but I also want a team who 'gets it.' A team that understands how implementing common strategies and reflecting on their impact will make them better teachers. I want a team that is eager to learn."

Coach: "So you're looking for a pilot team eager to implement common strategies because it will make them better teachers. Claire, tell me more about the feedback you want the pilot team to provide to you and the four team leaders. Do you have some specific points in mind?" *(summary and detail question)*

Claire: "As a matter of fact, yes. I do have some ideas about the feedback we need, but I haven't had a chance to think them all the way through. Up to this point, I've been thinking mostly about the process itself and the amount of time each step takes and how that works for them in the 45 minute time block available."

The above exchange between Claire and her coach illustrates the communication skills characteristic of Step 4. Notice that the coach discerns important ideas, brings them forward, and then adds the question or summary statements to expand and deepen understanding.

STEP 4 PITFALLS

Coaches certainly use the mutual understanding gained in Step 4 to uncover nuances of the coachees' current situation, but they also use them to inform and enable the next steps in the coaching conversation. Therefore, if coaches fail to fully employ the communication skills called for in this phase of coaching, the rest of the conversation will feel off-kilter to both the coach and the coachee.

While in Step 4 of the coaching conversation, which is where coaches and coachees seek to deepen understanding, coaches must avoid four common pitfalls.

Pitfall 1. Asking for Details or Clarification Out of a Voyeuristic Need to Know

The first pitfall, asking details out of a personal need to know, may be the result of bad habits developed over a lifetime of interacting with others without mindful intention about how to use conversations to be supportive and inspiring. Leaders who find themselves with a coach who asks questions that are not helpful to them or their situation may be working with a person who lacks the ability to maintain his or her coaching presence and role when the topic reminds one of his or her own interests, work, and life. Coaches who lose their coaching presence succumb to internal reactions that come up for them as they engage with coachees and listen to their stories (O'Neill, 2000).

Pitfall 2. Asking Questions Based on Past Personal Experiences Instead of From the Context of Coachees

Coaches who ask questions that reflect their past experiences assume their coachees' current situation is identical. Of course, this is never true. No matter how effective coaches were or are in educational leadership roles similar to their coachees, the milieu is completely different for their coachees: the people are different, the decisions are different, the data are different, the climates are different, and the roles their coachees have within the culture of their organizations are different.

To be helpful, coaching questions must always relate to the coachee's situations (Braun, 2009). Without thorough understanding of the coachee's perspective, coaches ask questions that are offtrack and irrelevant. What other choice do they have? If you do not truly understand the coachee's situation, through the eyes of the coachee, the questions you ask can only come from either a vague understanding of the situation, or from your own point of view. Off-kilter questions make coachees feel that the coach must have thrown a dart at a list of possible coaching questions and asked the one that the dart pierced.

Pitfall 3. Prematurely Introducing New Ideas

When coaches ask questions that introduce new ideas in Step 4, they have prematurely moved to Step 5. Worse, some coaches dispense with asking questions at all and just introduce new ideas as a way to surreptitiously slip in advice.

A coachee's response to the inquiries you put forth offers up essential data about their current situation, and it is from this response that you mindfully select your next coaching move. Coaches who give ideas to coachees in Step 4 may be operating from a belief that they know better than the coachee about what to do. This assumption flies in the face of the purpose of leadership coaching which is to draw out the wisdom of coachees so that they not only accomplish important work, but also deepen their *capacity* to accomplish great work. Thus, coaches who tell their coachees what to do short circuit the process of learning, and diminish the returns that coaching makes possible.

Pitfall 4. Rushing Coachees to Action

When in Step 4, coaches who rush coachees to action (Steps 6, 7, and 8) thrust them into problem-solving mode without the benefit of the rich thinking that arises out of the process of coaching. Think about how absurd this is from the perspective of coachees who come to coaching precisely because they need to wrestle with a vexing and complex situation where knowing what to do is neither obvious nor clear.

The easiest way to avoid this pitfall is to refrain from asking at this phase, "So, what could you do?" Your coachees may be too polite to say, but what they are thinking is "How the heck do I know? Do your coaching thing and maybe I'll figure that out!" Fear not my reader, you do ask this question in Steps 6 and 7, just not now.

READINESS FOR STEP 5

The minds of coaches actively seek to make sense of the stories told by their coachees. Coaches who rush Step 4 of the coaching conversation deprive themselves of the information and insight they need to appropriately summarize and paraphrase the coachee's descriptions, and to ask helpful clarifying and detail questions. This has a negative ripple effect on the rest of the coaching process, for if understanding is not achieved in Step 4, then coaches cannot ask excellent TLQs that provoke, excite, and engage the coachee at a completely different level in Step 5. The next chapter focuses entirely on the essential communication skills when asking TLQs.

Thought Leadership Questions

chapter 9

It is not the answer that enlightens, but the question.

—Eugene Ionesco (*Découvertes*, 1970, as quoted in *Choosing the Future: The Power of Strategic Thinking*, 1997, by Stuart Wells, p. 15)

Stimulating. Inspiring. Jarring. Intuitive. Imaginative. Provocative. Raucous. Insightful. I bet you never thought coaching could be so exciting! These words describe the effect that the coaching skills applied by coaches in Step 5 of the Powerful Coaching Conversation have on the mind of leaders as they "think" with a great coach at their side. How do great coaches catalyze breakthrough insights for the leaders they coach? They ask their coachees what I call *Thought Leadership Questions* (TLQs). Step 5 of the Powerful Coaching Conversation is when coaches ask TLQs they move from working with ideas and assumptions already in play (Step 4) to working with ideas that may become possibilities.

INSPIRED THOUGHT

If you have had the opportunity to coach colleagues engaged in passionate work, and if they ever said something to you along the lines of, "Now that's a good question," you were probably thrilled. Why thrilled? Because it most likely meant your coaching helped them wrestle with ideas they had not previously considered, but that contained tremendous value for their work (Stoltzfus, 2008).

As established in earlier chapters of this book, coaching is not the same thing as giving advice, or providing people with solutions. Nevertheless, coaching is a powerful leadership development strategy. In the hands of a skilled coach, TLQs catalyze deep, personal learning for the leader by producing flashes of insight (Johnson, 2010), those breakthrough "aha" moments that lead to inspired thought and purposeful action.

A COACHING SCENARIO: MEET "CAROLINE"

Caroline is one of four regional superintendents in a large urban school district, providing direct support and supervision to twenty principals. Until recently, Caroline played an active role not only in selecting the principals of the schools under her responsibility, but also in selecting the school administrative teams, including the assistant principals and deans. For years, the district superintendent supported the direct involvement of Caroline and her colleagues in selecting building administrators in their regions; this was the implicit cultural norm.

However, last year at the end of the school session, a new superintendent took over the district helm. During the summer that immediately followed, Caroline inferred from several examples that the new superintendent expected the principals, not the regional superintendents to make the final selection of the building administrative teams. The new superintendent did not directly convey this change in procedure to the regional superintendents. Instead, Caroline and her colleagues discovered what they began to assume was "the new process" when they ran into several principals exiting the human resources (HR) department, fresh and excited from filling out the paper work recommending their final candidate selection for the open administrator positions in their buildings.

Over Caroline's 15 years in the district she had worked hard to increase communication between the building principals and the central office, and she felt that real progress had been made, especially in the last two years. Therefore, she found the change in the administrative personnel selection process particularly distressing. In a session with her leadership coach, she expressed dismay that the changes brought in by the new superintendent would undermine and erode the recent gains in the quality and frequency of communication between building principals and the central office. Moreover, Caroline believed that without strong leadership from the regional superintendents in selecting the school administrative teams, essential information about the strengths and weaknesses of the candidates would not come up during the interview process. Caroline feared the result would be that the principals could find themselves in an untenable position down the road, having to work with individuals who may not be the right fit for their schools.

Although Caroline clearly was not a fan of the new process, which she believed the new superintendent preferred, she seemed surprisingly resigned to it. She told her coach that she wanted to focus the current coaching session on reframing her attitude toward the new process so that in Caroline's words, "I accept the new process and free my energy to focus on other issues where I *do* have power and influence."

ADDING STEP 5 TO THE POWERFUL COACHING CONVERSATION

Applying the Powerful Coaching Conversation, Caroline's coach first listened without interruption or judgment (Step 3), as Caroline told her story. Then when Caroline completed her narrative, her coach segued into Step 4 of the Powerful Coaching Conversation and asked clarifying and detail questions about the issues Caroline conveyed that were foremost on her mind and germane to her identified goal for the session ("to accept the new process and free my energy to focus on other issues where I *do* have power and influence").

Caroline's coach drew Step 4 to closure when she discerned that Caroline had completed her story and when vague concepts were clarified and crucial details were fleshed out. The coach achieved this by summarizing the issues, and then by making a segue statement to transition the coaching conversation into Step 5 (Step 5 is the sky blue color step on the Powerful Coaching Conversation protocol): "Let me ask you some thought leadership questions, and see where they take us." Here are samples of the questions Caroline's coach asked:

Sample Thought Leadership Questions for Caroline

- Caroline, you clarified earlier that the superintendent has never announced his approach as "the new process." In fact, you mentioned that you came to this conclusion based on observing some incidents. What stops you from asking the superintendent to clarify his expectations of your role in selecting the principal's administrative team?
- Caroline, what becomes possible if you accept that you no longer have a role in selecting the principal's leadership team? What is the best outcome these possibilities allow for you? For the principals? For the students and the district?
- How does the new administrative personnel selection process impact the most important goals you have for the schools you are accountable for?
- Where do you still have influence in the building level administrative personnel selection process? What are the characteristics of the principals who would be most likely to invite that influence?

In reality, even with the identical coachee and the identical situation, no two coaches would ask the same TLQs at the same place in the conversation, or in the same way. For example, a different leadership coach might have asked Caroline these TLQs:

- Caroline, what if you *did* still have influence and power in the administrative personnel selection process? What would you have revised about the old process?
- Caroline, what do you want to learn, or what do you believe you have to learn in order to make the new process work? What do you want the principals to learn?

THE MAGIC OF THOUGHT LEADERSHIP QUESTIONS: HOW THE MIND WORKS

In his terrific 2010 book, *Where Good Ideas Come From*, Steve Johnson writes about the extraordinary process of the human mind as it arrives at inspired thought. In some cases, such as during the development of the World Wide Web, the progression toward insight takes longer than you might think, sometimes involving years of incubation before the right bits of information connect and take form.

Johnson says, "Good ideas are not conjured out of thin air; they are built out of a collection of existing parts the composition of which expands (and occasionally contracts) over time" (2010, p. 15). Coaches who have the pleasure of coaching leaders through a series of conversations focused on long-term projects regularly witness their coachees assemble "existing parts" into the good ideas described by Johnson. But, even a single coaching conversation provides a microversion of the same process. In fact, the Powerful Coaching Conversation protocol is specifically engineered with built-in incubation time precisely for this reason; to allow ideas to spark and connect with what the leader knows as well as with what has been (up to this point) outside of the leader's perceptions.

Thought Leadership Questions Lead to Thoughtful Leadership

TLQs are tangential, but strategically essential to leadership success. They draw the mind toward an eclectic array of connected, but imperceptible information that enable leaders to think systemically and beyond their limited perspective.

In Step 5, the attention of leaders is captured for a while by the organizational and personal context surrounding the situation, which may exist in blind spots outside of their current perspectives; TLQs flood the mind with light and illuminate ground that the leader did not previously see. At times, this territory is blindingly obvious to the coach, and therefore seems curiously missing from the leader's narrative. But, great coaches know that this is how it is with the wonderful human mind: we all draw inimitable conclusions based on the selective data we each decide warrants our attention. This tendency makes each person delightfully unique, but because our minds are wired to see what we expect to see, it also creates blind spots that become liabilities.

Great coaches ask TLQs that positively presume their coachees have knowledge about the issues raised (Costa & Garmston, 1994), and they validate coachees as lively, willing, and even wise originators of action in their work (Allison & Reeves, 2012). For example, Caroline's coach asked, *"Caroline what do you want to learn, or what do you believe you have to learn in order to make the new process work? What do you want the principals to learn?"* These questions do not ask Caroline *if* she knows what she and the principals should learn, they *assume* she knows something about this topic, and they invite her to organize her thoughts and express them aloud so that she and the coach can continue to work with them during this coaching conversation.

Effective TLQs acknowledge the leadership abilities of coachees, and they extend the mind toward the essential wisdom of disciplines surrounding the work. For example, recall that Caroline's coach asked her, *"Caroline, what becomes possible if you accept that you no longer have a role in selecting the principal's leadership team? What is the best outcome these possibilities allow for you? For the principals? For the students and the district?"* From these questions we can infer that Caroline's coach knows a thing or two about employee engagement and accountability—especially the idea that when people know they are accountable for outcomes, they tend to be more engaged and proactive in the process—and quite possibly drew on this knowledge to formulate these queries. Although the coach does not know how Caroline will think through these questions, by drawing her attention to this important territory in human behavior in organizations, it is quite possible that Caroline will recognize that one outcome could be increased accountability on the part of the principals for the development and performance of the team members they select.

TLQs also draw leaders into fields of inquiry where they can safely bump up against ideas they may find threatening, or toward issues in the organization or in their leadership style that may be tough to examine, let alone talk about. For example, when her coach asked, "Caroline, what stops you from asking the superintendent to clarify his expectations of your role in selecting the principal's administrative team?" Caroline paused, looked downward, and took a deep breath. She then told her coach, "I guess I'm afraid that I'll either offend him, or put myself on his radar screen in a way that I really don't want. What it really comes down to is that I have a tendency to make people defensive when I ask questions of them."

Coaches Lead With Thought Leadership Questions

Every now and then, a novice coach in one of my workshops will ask me, "Hey Elle, how the heck is it 'leadership coaching' if coaches can't give advice, offer opinions, provide solutions, or share their personal bias and experience? What's left for the coach to do? Where's the leadership?"

The confusion about "where the leadership is in leadership coaching" is especially strong in cultures where "leadership" is equated with having answers—not with asking questions. The cultures of many organizations are steeped in beliefs and practices that favor quick responses and "putting out fires" over reflection and leadership development. Often, the people surrounding leaders and experts do not ask questions. Under the worst of conditions, they are either cowed into submission by the leader's charisma or bullying style, or they are sycophants who try to figure out what the leaders want to hear, and then stick to acceptable scripts in order to not to fall out of favor. Leaders are dangerously isolated in their leadership responsibilities without colleagues who ask good questions of them. TLQs, on the other hand, often take on the interests of various stakeholders and shareholders in the system, causing leaders to consider different points of view and forcing them to think about how their behavior and decisions impact others.

TLQs are intuitively indispensible to the conversation and as such, can be jarring to the leader when the coach asks them. TLQs make coachees do double takes, raise eyebrows, look at their coaches with quizzical respect or irritation, and even smack themselves in the forehead with the palms of their hands, and say things like, *"that's* a good question" or "I wonder why I didn't think of that?"

TLQs are provocative in that they rattle the mind by asking leaders to consider something *more* than what they were thinking, or *less* than what they were thinking, or something completely *different* from what they were thinking. For example, a coach who asks the question: *"What would you change about the process of administrator selection if you still had power and influence?"* trains the focus of the conversation on ideal processes in administrator selection and away from whether or not the leader has the power and influence to make those changes. TLQs can also be evocative; they cause coachees to see themselves in the story and they bring out emotions, for example, *"What are you most optimistic about as you see yourself carrying out the new procedures?"*

The cognitive dissonance that results from provocative and evocative TLQs causes leaders to consider different ideas, thereby increasing the scope of their perspective. At the same time, they afford coaches the opportunity to lead by navigating the conversation toward essential territory currently outside of the leader's awareness (Marquardt, 2005). Coaches who skillfully use TLQs assist to elevate discussions between people in the organization by changing the focus from habitual ways of thinking that lead to clichéd ideas, to inspired moments that accelerate innovation.

Ownership, Action, Accountability

TLQs are not necessarily designed for coachees to "answer," but rather they are to prompt reflection. They are all about the coachee—not the coach: *"Maria, what do you see are the possibilities?"* By including the word "you," TLQs empower leaders by causing them to first access and then draw on their previous experiences and knowledge base. Once a coach asks a TLQ, it now belongs to the coachee; the coach cannot predict how the coachee wrestles with any given TLQ.

Powerful TLQs embody concepts from organizational learning, adult learning, and other related fields of inquiry, and even though coaches ask TLQs for good reasons that are justified by the coachee's focus, they always inspire unique insight. Therefore, coachees "own" the insights that emerge from the pieces of information that organize and connect as a result of the coaching process. TLQs foreshadow relevant possibilities that crystallize in later stages of the coaching conversation, and are precursors to arguably one of the most powerful outcomes of leadership coaching—effective action.

USING THOUGHT LEADERSHIP QUESTIONS FOR GOOD

Educational leaders who work with a leadership coach usually do not squander their coaching sessions on trifling matters, or simple items on their "to do" list that they may or may not feel motivated to accomplish. On the contrary, leaders who work with a coach are usually in pursuit of aspirational goals that will make a difference for their organization. Therefore, great leadership coaches ask TLQs to remind these leaders who they are and what matters to them.

Coaches must be careful not to slip into advising, or worse yet, manipulating coachees toward ideas, actions, and outcomes that the coach is biased toward, or that the coach believes is the best course of action. Instead, the coach asks TLQs that are in service of the coachee's project, and the goal the coachee wants to accomplish in this coaching session.

Great coaches recognize the responsibility they have to ask TLQs that focus the attention of leaders on what they want to achieve. Knowing that careless coaching questions take people away from where they want to go, great coaches look at the questions they ask and check themselves on the motivation and intention behind them. A few of the pitfalls that leadership coaches avoid when asking TLQs are:

1. Asking questions out of anxiety and worry for the leader, which cause the leader to stream energy to the wrong things. For example, lets say the leader you are coaching has to defend a decision that displeased a large number of stakeholders. As coach, you need to set aside your personal anxiety about this challenge and resist asking questions that prevent the leader from seeing other points of view, or that make the leader feel shaky and less resilient.

2. Asking questions to subtly manipulate the coachee in a direction the coach feels is best (as opposed to the direction that the coachee feels is best). Coaches who forget that their role is to partner in thought with leaders who want to produce certain outcomes can inadvertently derail their coachees with questions that undermine their momentum.

For example, I once had a conversation with an educator who as a highly paid consultant fancied himself as an expert in all aspects of educational leadership. The problem is that he also presented himself as a coach. On one occasion, this individual casually mentioned to me that he was about to "do a coaching call in order to convince a principal not to pursue a specific strategy"—a strategy that the consultant felt was flawed. In trying to steer the leader, he was "coaching" in a different direction; this coach presumed that he knew better than the leader knew for himself. This coach forgot that coaching conversations are not theoretical or philosophical chats. Because coaching conversations always end with the leader taking action in the real world, the questions asked of leaders during coaching sessions will create reality. Coaches have to ask themselves whether the reality they are helping their coachee create is the actual reality of the coachee's aspirations.

3. Asking questions to surreptitiously give advice and make recommendations. Coaches who struggle with releasing their personal net of memory (discussed at length in Chapter 7, *Listen, Just Listen*) are full of advice and ideas that, without vigilance, find their way into Step 5 in the form of questions. Usually, coaches are individuals who have great reputations for being leaders themselves. In education, leadership coaches may be current employees or retirees from the same system where they coach. These leaders are knowledgeable, successful, and wise. Yet, even with all of their experience, these coaches do not walk in the shoes of the leaders they coach. They may think that they know all the ins and outs of the system, but the truth is, the system has changed—at least we hope it has changed! The people have changed, the context has changed, the tools have changed, the politics have changed, regulations have changed, the community has changed.

Let's face it, systems are alive and changing all the time. Coaches who ask questions in order to sneak in their own advice, opinions, and lessons from their past experiences ask questions that are irrelevant to the coachee, and therefore are not in service of either the coachee or their ultimate progress.

4. Asking questions that start with the word "why." Questions that start with the word "Why" throw people into the past and undermine resilience (Allison & Reeves, 2012). Think about this example: *"Why did you decide to move forward with reorganizing the high school campus into teams?"* At the very least, this question will cause the coachee to use valuable coaching time to respectfully explain their decision to you. More harmful, this question could thrust the coachee into justifying the decision to your satisfaction, or blaming others for their role in the decision, or denying that they made the decision at all. Remember, the goal of coaching is action that makes a difference for the organization. Questions that start with the word "why" take the leader out of the power that exists in the present moment, which is where the actions of leaders have an impact.

DEEP WELLS OF KNOWLEDGE

In spite of the foundational perspective that coaching is *not* advising or telling people what to do, leaders who coach cannot disguise the richness of who they are as leaders. Nor would we want them to. So, how do coaches use their knowledge and experience in ways that are appropriate to the role of coaching? Step 5 of the Powerful Coaching Conversation is a time for coaches to lead through their TLQs. When I look out at a room filled with effective leaders, I can't help but feel awe and respect for the depth of experience and wisdom before me. Every leader draws on and integrates knowledge, skills, dispositions, and abilities to accomplish great work. The questions asked by coaches, by virtue of the TLQs they select, are not designed to sneak in advice, opinions, and judgments. Nor are they motivated by manipulation and anxiety-based impulses. Rather they draw on the coach's deep wells of knowledge, which inform and govern the reasons behind their selections. With effective TLQs, the bursts of creativity and insight that emerge during Step 5, bring coachees to a new plane of thought where options are suddenly visible and possibilities for the organization expand.

In the next chapter, we look at the final three steps of the Powerful Coaching Conversation, where coachees determine where they can take action, define and redefine the possibilities, and finally commit to specific actions to move their project forward.

The Jaunty Walk

chapter 10

Action is the antidote to despair.

—Joan Baez (*Rolling Stone Magazine*, April 13, 1983)

Some years ago, I read something that referred to the Dalai Lama as "a great coach," and on that recommendation I saw a film called *Ten Questions for the Dalai Lama*. In several scenes, I saw His Holiness visiting remote mountain villages, or crowded village squares where lines of people snaked endlessly through the streets, each person waiting to meet with their spiritual leader. Close-ups of the faithful revealed just how emotional these meetings were for them. Many wore sad and troubled expressions, the hardships and sufferings of a difficult life traced in the lines of their faces.

For his part, the Dalai Lama mostly wore his famous smile with his crinkly, smiley eyes. But, in his initial greetings of individuals, the expressions on his face especially caught my attention. Uncannily, they mirrored the unique emotions on the face of each person he met. When a happy, eager person approached him, the Dalai Lama flung his arms wide and laughed out loud. Similarly, when a person approached bent over, weeping with sadness, the Dalai Lama transformed his face and body to look the same. He would bend forward, hands clasped at his heart, don a compassionate frown and wipe at his eyes; then he would take the person in his arms, or he would grip their hands. The pair would first exchange a few words. Then the Dalai Lama would stand taller, throw his head back, and laugh. Inevitably, his followers stood taller, threw their heads back, and laughed, too.

No matter how sad their initial demeanor, after their time with the Dalai Lama the individuals left with a bounce in their step. They strode away with their heads held high and chests flung forward. For all the world, they looked unburdened and empowered to make great things happen in their lives. Later, when I described what I had seen to a friend, I called it a "jaunty walk," and I understood that great coaching needs to produce something similar for all involved in the process.

THE JAUNTY WALK

Steps 6, 7, and 8 of the Powerful Coaching Conversation produce the jaunty walk. Spinning into motion quickly, fueled by the often stunning insights derived from exploring the Thought Leadership Questions offered by their coaches in Step 5, coachees suddenly see possibilities, where before they saw limitations. But more importantly, they understand what they *can* do and they feel empowered to go forth and take action.

Coaches must listen well and scribble reasonably legible notes during this phase as the steps tend to work together quickly, and often out of order. And, as always, they must take care to listen without interrupting, or otherwise derail the momentum of the coachees' thought processes.

Although Steps 6, 7, and 8 often merge together, coaches must understand what each step is designed to produce, and mindfully facilitate their use in the process. Take a moment to review the colorful version of the Powerful Coaching Conversation Transfer Tool at this time, and you will remember that these three steps in the process (presented in dark green and in Step 8, as white surrounded by dark green) celebrate and leverage the wisdom of coachees and encourage them to step into their work and lives with enlightened action.

Step 6. Generative Thinking

Thinking back to the story about the Dalai Lama, during Step 6 in the Powerful Coaching Conversation, coachees straighten up, lean forward, smile, and with insight flashing in their eyes, suddenly seem to see their way through whatever confusion or uncertainty they might have initially felt. In reality, the insights that visit coachees in Step 6 are not sudden at all. They come from everything the leader knows, has experienced, and is motivated to learn, teach, and change about the world around them.

Possibilities Emerge

The engineering of the Powerful Coaching Conversation, combined with the skill and intuition of the coach, facilitates and catalyzes the process. In Step 6, drawing on theories of generative thinking (Wittrock, 1992), leaders see meaningful relationships between the ideas, stories, and experiences that surfaced throughout Steps 1 through 5.

Wittrock, who first formulated the model of generative thinking, writes, "At the essence of this functional model are the generative learning processes that people use actively and dynamically to (a) selectively attend to events, and (b) generate meaning for events by constructing relations between new or incoming information and previously acquired information, concepts, and background knowledge" (1992, p. 532). Applying generative thinking to leadership, authors of the book *Generative Leadership: Shaping New Futures for Today's Schools* write: "Generative leaders are intent on bringing to light new possibilities for action and growth" (Klimek, Ritzenhein, & Sullivan, 2008, p. 6). Every aspect of the Powerful Coaching Conversation comes together in these last three steps to expose possibilities and to illuminate the way forward.

Initiating Step 6

Coaches launch Step 6 by asking some form of these questions: *"Given our conversation up to this point, what are you thinking now? Where do you want to take action? What would that make possible for you, for others, and for the organization?"* Although coaches are not required to ask all of these questions at once, I often do. When I lay all of these questions on the table at the same time, it is with the coachee's understanding that they may choose to work any one of them, and in any order they please.

Acknowledge the Shift

Consider for a moment what it means for coaches to ask coachees: *"Where are you now in your thinking?"* Or *"What are you thinking now?"* Do you see that the words acknowledge and assume that coachees have changed? That during the span of 30 or 50 minutes, they have accessed wisdom within themselves that maybe they never knew was there? Step 6 acknowledges this shift and signals coachees to transition from thinking primarily about the current state of their project to identifying where it could go next. When coaches ask, "Now what are you thinking?" they respectfully acknowledge that the thoughts of the leader have evolved.

Step 7. Brainstorming Options

In Step 7 of the Powerful Coaching Conversation, coaches invite coachees to generate ideas about what they think they could do. At this point, the ideas brought forth foreshadow the actions that coachees will ultimately commit to in Step 8. They also continue to surface new possibilities within the system. In fact, as seen by the Powerful Coaching Conversation protocol, coachees often move fluidly back and forth between Steps 6 and 7.

Initiating Step 7

Coaches initiate Step 7 by asking something to this effect: *"What could you do in the area where you want to take action? In the time between now and our next coaching conversation, what could you do?"* As coachees brainstorm possibilities, the role of the coach is to take notes, listen, summarize, and ask relevant clarifying and detail questions that help coachees sort out the benefits of their ideas. Coaches might also bring forward additional and relevant information from previous conversations, which seem absent from the brainstorming. For example, they might say something like, *"Fabiana, I'm remembering something you said last month about how important it is to provide your director with two or three research articles whenever you make a recommendation. Is that relevant to what you are thinking about in this case?"*

A pitfall for coaches in this phase of the coaching conversation is to put forth a bunch of ideas *they* have about what their coachees should do. Coaches who use Step 7 to share and suggest their own ideas disempower their coachees and undermine the goals of coaching. While processing Step 7, coaches can better serve coachees by using their great coaching skills: listening, summarizing, probing for clarification and details, prompting thought leadership, and voicing related systemic experiences from the coachee's own system.

Step 8. Wisdom and Commitment to Action

One of my favorite coaching quotes comes from Joan Baez who said, "Action is the antidote to despair." Without action, leadership coaching is nothing more than a series of theoretical conversations or friendly chit-chats. Without action, good leaders who want to do meaningful work that can make a difference for students and the community are frustrated; they lose energy and begin to feel inefficient and ineffective.

The final moments of the Powerful Coaching Conversation end with the coachee's commitment to carry out one to three of the actions brainstormed in Step 7. Coaches ask, *"What will you do? What actions will you take between now and our next coaching conversation in order to move your project forward?"* The commitment required of coachees at this point is to *initiate* these actions, not necessarily complete them, between now and the next coaching conversation. Of course, the next coaching session begins with a reference to the commitments made at the end of the previous session, and an invitation to the coachee to update the coach, provide a current status of the actions and the overall project, and describe how it all played out.

No Second-Guessing

Coaches must take care not to undermine all the hard work that led to this moment of commitment by disagreeing with or second-guessing the wisdom of their coachees' decisions. Why should they? When coaches mindfully engage in the science of coaching, they can trust that their coachees move forward in the important work they do with insight and confidence. Aside from resonating belief and confidence in your coachees at the end of the coaching conversation, there are also strategies in Step 8 on how to show additional support. The two strategies provided below are not mandatory. Coaches can use them whenever they believe they will be useful to a specific coachee:

- For each commitment, ask coachees to foreshadow challenges that might come up and then how they could prevent them from occurring. This question validates that you want them to stay on track toward their goal and allows them to imagine ways to confront barriers to that success.
- After coachees affirm one to three commitments to action, coaches may offer resources or tools to support them, but coachees are under no obligation to use them or even look at them! It is important that coaches take care not to add actions to their coachees' commitments, and must certainly not take liberty with this allowance by thrusting their agenda on the coachees.

Once coachees are clear on the one to three actions they want to take, coaches could also ask their coachees to send them a quick memo or text message when they accomplish them. For example: *"Hi Elle—just wanted you to know the scheduled meeting went great today! Will tell you about it during our call on Thursday."*

You're Going to Be Great

In the last moments of the coaching session, coaches resonate faith in the leadership of their coachees and send them off with compassion. Realizing their coachees are reentering their work and lives with a transformed perspective, coaches reinforce the coachees' confidence about taking action. You'll find your own way and your own words for expressing this to your coachees, but I always say, "You're going to be great."

A COACHING SCENARIO: MEET "ADAM"

"Adam" was assistant superintendent of curriculum and instruction in a medium-size urban school district. Three years ago, Adam asked me to coach him on a project that was near and dear to his heart. He wanted to form an alliance with the state university to make his district a welcoming and rigorous destination for student teachers. His goal was to see his district acknowledged for providing extraordinary support for student teachers, under the guidance of the most exceptional teachers available. His vision included the idea that a number of the student teachers would ultimately accept teaching positions within the district once they graduated from the university. He saw this program partnership as an important first step in the district leadership development program.

During one particularly memorable coaching session, Adam asked to focus on ways to involve his colleagues in the decisions he would soon make to structure the new student teacher program. Adam said, "It isn't that the other members of the leadership team and the mentor teachers don't believe this is a good idea, but they see it more as a continuation of what we already do. I'd like them to work with me to develop a new student teacher program that develops everyone and produces more benefits—for student teachers, the mentors, the university, and most importantly for our students."

During Steps 1, 2, and 3 of our coaching conversation, Adam expanded on his ideas while I listened and took notes. He expressed a few thoughts that struck me as important to his project:

- "The gist of the project as it stands—to provide mentors for student teachers in collaboration with the university—does not significantly disrupt, challenge, or change the lives of most teachers and administrators, one way or the other."
- "It's a little discordant that while one of our major district initiatives is to close the achievement gaps, our mentor teachers who are considered 'the best' are assigned to the AP classes with 'the best' students."
- "Several of the teachers I have in mind as the program mentors are ready for new challenges."

When Adam completed everything he wanted to say up to this point, I segued the coaching conversation into Step 4 by offering this summary: "Adam, from what you've said, you envision a student teacher mentor program that breaks the mold. You described several components: a strong relationship with the university, student teachers who learn from the best mentor teachers, and eventually accept teaching positions in the district. At the same time, you observe that the mentors are not assigned to classes that challenge them to develop teaching practices that help everyone learn how to reach struggling students and close achievement gaps." Adam agreed with my summary, especially the part about breaking the mold and the incoherence between mentor teacher class assignments and the district initiative. Then, still in Step 4, I asked Adam several detail and clarification questions:

- "You said you wanted to focus this conversation on how to involve more people in the decisions you need to make to structure this project. What are the decisions you need to make?"
- "Tell me more about the mentor teachers you have in mind in relationship to the district initiative to close the achievement gap."
- "You mentioned that you thought some of the existing mentor teachers were ready for new challenges. What else do you know about that? Can you give me some examples?"
- "You mentioned the disconnect between the district initiative and the mentor teacher class assignments. Say more about how classroom assignments are made in the district."
- "You envision a strong relationship with the university. What are the details around that vision from your perspective? What about from the perspective of the university?"

What I want you to notice about the questions I asked Adam in Step 4 is that they all invite him to more deeply explore the topics he put on the table. As he does so, both he and I more clearly see the forces in play within the ecosystem of his organization. Some of these forces appear as policies and practices, others come from the culture, and what people in the system expect. As Adam worked with the detail and clarification questions I asked in Step 4, he began to make these observations about his project:

1. The university expects the district to immerse their student teachers in practices grounded in crucial educational research, including focusing on student learning through meaningful and frequent feedback, providing multiple opportunities to learn, and designing project-based learning experiences.

2. The teacher assignment process in the district is strongly rooted in practices and a culture that place the most experienced teachers in the "best" classes.

3. Several existing mentor teachers, but not all, are "go getters" who participate in all of the professional development offered by the district related to closing achievement gaps.

4. Aside from occasional bubbles of teachers who retire at the same time, the largest numbers of teacher turnover and attrition take place in the first three years of employment. Adam says these novice teachers are "overwhelmed," and don't always feel prepared or supported to help struggling students succeed.

After a while, I transitioned Adam into Step 5 of the coaching conversation. I said, "Adam, you've illuminated some important issues around your project. Now, let me put some thought leadership questions on the table for you to work with." Here are the questions I offered Adam:

- "How do you imagine mentor teachers and student teachers making a powerful impact for students?"
- "What does being a teacher leader mean in your district?"
- "What does it mean to be a mentor teacher in education?"

As Adam worked with the ideas conveyed within these TLQs, he expressed several new thoughts, including that the opportunity to partner with the university would be wasted if it did not include leadership in closing achievement gaps. He recognized the existing barriers around changing teacher assignments, but he had at least three mentor teachers who were open to assignments that placed them with student teachers in "high need" classes. He also talked about the support these teachers would require from the district and the necessity that they keep their eyes on the bigger picture of building teacher leaders—leaders who make a difference and feel committed to grow within the district.

I always wish conversations like this one with Adam could be filmed! He was excited by the possibilities he was beginning to see and he scribbled out a rough diagram showing the flow of how he might proceed. His eyes were flashing with insight and he leaned forward to explain his ideas to me. His body language and speech conveyed optimism and confidence.

Adam had taken the conversation into Steps 6, 7, and 8 of the Powerful Coaching Conversation; he was more than ready to do the jaunty walk.

I said, "Adam tell me what you are thinking now—where do you want to start to involve others in the decisions that will shape this program?" Notice that this question brings Adam back to the goals of this coaching session. Adam said that he saw an opportunity to work with key people to look at how they could reconfigure a few of the mentor/student teacher pairings around classrooms where they could engage in action research about real ways to help struggling students learn. He saw no reason to disconnect the student teacher program from the goals of the district and indeed, from the larger needs facing society and the field of education. Adam said, "If we really want to be leaders, we can't waste this opportunity to make a difference for our most vulnerable students."

I then asked Adam to brainstorm. "Then, what could you do next, Adam? What are the possibilities?" Here is what he rattled off:

- I could ask Human Resources (HR) to help me work around the way we've always made teacher assignments.
- I could have an initial conversation with the two mentor teachers I'm considering and see how they react to new assignments that put them with struggling classes, and not just the AP classes.
- I need to learn more about what is known about closing achievement gaps.
- I could meet with the university person to get a better idea about their expectations for student teachers.
- I could talk with the teachers currently assigned to the classes I'm thinking about. A few of them would make fine mentor teachers too—even though we have never tapped them for that role.

After a few minutes of brainstorming, I said, "Adam, you see a lot of possibilities here. Let me ask you, out of all these ideas, what will you do between now and our next coaching session?" Adam said, "I think I'll start with the conversations with the mentor teachers who I believe would be open to change. But, I also need to do the same thing with the teachers who already work with struggling students. I'm embarrassed to say I never thought of them as mentors for student teachers before now. I think I'll run a few things past the HR person, too. However, I'll have to think carefully about how to talk with her because she gets nervous when we talk about teacher reassignment, and I don't want her to make up her mind too quickly."

This coaching session was now at the end, and Adam was ready to reenter his work world with a transformed perspective about his work, the people around him, and about himself. Certainly, his project still had a long way to go and along the way, he would experience all sorts of interesting twists and turns, opportunities, windfalls, and challenges. But, my goodness he is undertaking good and meaningful work.

Adam and I stood together and shook hands. I told him, "Adam, I know you are going to be great." After Adam exited the conference room, I peered around the corner of the door and saw him striding down the hallway, grinning ear to ear and high-fiving colleagues and students in greeting as they passed. Yep, Adam was doing the jaunty walk.

Part IV

Progress

Monitoring the Results of Leadership Coaching

chapter 11

The pure and simple truth is rarely pure and never simple.

—Oscar Wilde (*The Importance of Being Earnest*, 1895, Act I)

Just as with any organizational strategy, leaders at the helm of leadership coaching programs need to know if they are producing the desired effects. Hence, the goal of this chapter is to provide you with some approaches to consider for measuring the effectiveness of your leadership coaching initiative.

One of my favorite questions to ask leaders and decision makers when we talk about monitoring indicators of successful leadership coaching is this: What could happen if more leaders in your organization supported other leaders in accomplishing the most important goals? In education, the answers paint a promising picture:

- "We would retain our best principals."
- "Teacher effectiveness would increase."
- "Employees would be engaged and enjoy coming to work."
- "People would feel less alone and more connected to each other."
- "We would develop better leaders from within our teaching ranks."
- "Student achievement would improve."

Each one of the responses bulleted above suggest data that could be used to measure the impact of your leadership coaching program. With just a little more specificity, each response can be fleshed out with both quantitative and qualitative data. For the examples presented above, and before you go any further into this chapter, list the data sources from within your own system that you could use to verify the expressed results. For this exercise, respond instinctively—without worrying about being "right." What are the data sources you identified? Does your list include these examples?

- The percentage of principals who have been in the district for four years or more.
- The percentage of teachers whose students demonstrate mastery of important standards.
- The percentage of employees who take leadership roles in important district and school projects.
- The number of employees holding coaching conversations during the workday.
- The percentage of district teachers who become teacher leaders, assistant principals, and principals.
- The percentage of students at proficiency level or higher in reading, writing, math, science, or other areas.

Leaders expect leadership coaching to empower them to have an even greater and more precise impact on their selected goals than if they did the same work without a leadership coach. This expectation leads us to two primary areas of focus for evaluation, which are best expressed as questions:

1. Is the leadership coaching program and process operating as expected?

2. Do leaders with coaches create results for the organization?

The answers to these two overarching questions provide interested stakeholders with feedback about the implementation of the coaching program, and about the impact coached leaders have on the goals of their organization. The process begins with identifying a few key indicators for each, and monitoring them over time. We begin with examining specific indicators to validate if your leadership coaching program and the inherent process is working.

IS LEADERSHIP COACHING OPERATING AS EXPECTED?

Before organizations reap the intended benefits of coaching, the leadership coaching program itself must be actively operating. In other words, you need to know that coaches are coaching, and leaders are engaged in coaching and consider it valuable. When it comes to evaluating if the leadership coaching process is working, you already have two key tools in place that work in tandem to make the intangible more tangible: the Coaching Agreement, and the First 100-Day Plan.

Feedback Inherent in the Coaching Agreement and the First 100-Day Plan

Used together, the Coaching Agreement and the First 100-Day Plan suggest several important indicators for evaluating leadership coaching program implementation. If you are a leadership coach, you can track these indicators for each of the leaders you coach. If you are an organizational leader in charge of your system's leadership coaching strategy, you can ask each leadership coach to send this information to you so you can aggregate it. Better yet, set up a program (such as survey monkey), which creates and publishes online surveys, and ask coaches to upload their individual data at regular intervals.

Throughout Coaching Engagements

For purposes of program evaluation, coaches and leaders of coaching programs should seek information from coachees about what elements of the coaching system are helpful (Vanderburg & Stephens, 2010), and how they view the impact of the coaching project on the organization. For example, we can easily ask leaders who have been coached to rate the extent to which they took action in their project to achieve specific milestones. We can also ask leaders who have been coached to rate the relationship between their project and important changes in the organization.

Here are the indicators that arise naturally out of the Coaching Agreement and the First 100-Day Plan:

- The number/percentage of leaders participating in leadership coaching.
- The number of coaching conversations taking place per month, or per quarter (e.g., per coachee, overall, and per building).
- The percentage of occasions when leaders agree that the coaching conversation empowered them to achieve the goals they identified at the start of the conversation. This feedback also provides powerful formative feedback to coaches, which allows them to refine their use of the Powerful Coaching Conversation protocol.
- The percentage of leadership projects that primarily serve established organizational goals (e.g., district goals, school goals, department or division goals—whichever are closest and most relevant to the coachee's project).

Each of the indicators bulleted above are relatively easy to capture, either by coaches or coachees, as part of carrying out the long-term coaching engagement.

At the End of Coaching Engagements

The final coaching conversation between coaches and their coachees provides a time for celebration, reflection, and feedback. Even if the coach and coachee plan to continue their coaching relationship by starting a new coaching agreement, coaches and leaders find great value in holding a final conversation that renders additional feedback about how the leadership coaching initiative is working. Conducted as an oral or written survey, the following six questions convey key assumptions about what leadership coaching is designed to produce. The results of this fairly quick "end of engagement survey" help distinguish quality coaching from poor coaching. To make these key assumptions of leadership coaching more tangible, ask your coachees to respond to the questions below with answers ranging from **strongly agree, agree, neither, disagree, or strongly disagree.** Additionally, invite coachees to provide supplementary information or examples:

1. Through my position, my leadership project contributed to the goals of my organization.

2. I reached the milestones of my project sooner with a coach than I would have if I had not been working with a coach.

3. My confidence in leading my project increased as a result of coaching.

4. I've grown in leadership skills, knowledge, and attitudes as a result of being coached throughout this project.

5. In the course of my leadership on this project, I've worked with others and have helped them develop as leaders.

6. My organization benefitted from the actions I took to launch and implement my project.

Securing data on the implementation of your leadership coaching strategy and how it is working for coaches and the leaders they coach is one piece of the puzzle. The second piece of the puzzle is linking leadership coaching to organizational results, including student achievement.

DO LEADERS WITH COACHES CREATE RESULTS FOR THE ORGANIZATION?

You may recall the Wallace Foundation study on leadership referenced in Chapter 2, and specifically the finding that "Leadership is second only to classroom instruction among all school related factors that contribute to what students learn at schools." As indirect as the idea might feel at first, the link between leadership and student achievement helps us understand how to evaluate the impact of leadership coaching on the organization. For if leadership affects student achievement, and if leadership coaching develops leaders, then the value of leadership coaching is made visible by tangible indicators that already exist within the ecosystem of the organization, including student achievement indicators.

A Scenario

Let's go back to the story of Carrie and Sarah, the two regional superintendents from Chapter 1 whose shared leadership coaching project was to initiate *leadership success plans* as a strategy for serving the larger district and board goals, which were "to develop principal leadership capacity throughout the district." When Carrie and Sarah mapped out the First 100-Days for launching their project, they also identified a few indicators that would give them feedback about the success of their project as it relates to leadership development in the district.

Project Indicators

Project indicators give project leaders good feedback that initiatives are underway. These indicators can often be updated monthly and are easily tracked. However, because they are unique to each coachee's project, the leaders you coach may have to invent ways to collect and display the data. For example, Carrie and Sarah wanted to see more of the principals developing leadership success plans based on areas that either they perceived as needing improvement, or areas that Carrie and Sarah identified for them. Here is the indicator they decided to track:

- The percentage of principals who had a leadership success plan linked to the district administrator evaluation. Carrie and Sarah kept track of this statistic simply by maintaining a spreadsheet of the principals they supervised and how many of them had developed a leadership success plan linked to their previous evaluation.

Organizational Indicators

Organizational indicators show that valued conditions within the organization are improving or sustaining high levels of performance. These data usually already exist within the ecosystem of the organization, sometimes in departments and subsystems that are different from the leaders. For example, Carrie and Sarah decided that if more school principals were successful leaders, they in turn would produce even more successful leaders from within the teaching and administrative ranks of their schools who would then remain in the district and lend their leadership in other capacities. They also thought that these successful principals would foster a climate and culture that promoted great teaching and learning. Fueled by these thoughts, Carrie and Sarah made the decision to track these additional indicators:

- The percentage of principals with leadership success plans who also recommend administrators and teachers in their schools for more demanding leadership positions in the district. Good news for Carrie and Sarah! The Human Resources office already tracks this information and was more than happy to provide these data to them on a quarterly basis.
- The percentage of principals with leadership success plans where 95% of their school culture and climate assessments are rated at a 3 or 4 by stakeholders (with a 3 rating indicating very good, and a 4 rating signifying excellent). In Carrie and Sarah's district, school climate surveys are conducted by principals three times per year.

Student Achievement Indicators

Finally, Carrie and Sarah decided to link their project to the academic area most in need of strong leadership: reading and writing performance for all students. To tighten and emphasize this link, they asked all principals who had developed a leadership success plan to focus on their leadership development through programs and initiatives within their schools, in order to increase reading and writing application across curricula. As with the organizational indicators above, the indicators that Carrie and Sarah needed to monitor for this focus already existed in the ecosystem of the organization in the form of state and district assessments. Moreover, mechanisms for their collection and dissemination were in place and carried out by the office of assessment and accountability. Carrie and Sarah only needed to request a report, and then make their own correlations to those principals with leadership success plans.

Link Back to Coaching

Let's return to the original premise that leadership is linked to student achievement and leadership coaching is a strategy for developing leaders. When indicators show that the coaching process is working as expected and that the indicators selected by coachees are trending toward desired goals, it is fair to say that coaching is a worthy initiative for leadership development.

On a larger scale, if you are a leader at the helm of a leadership coaching initiative for a system (district, region, state, national), you may want to find an approach, such as a dashboard, scorecard, or even a simple bar graph, to visually link increased implementation of leadership coaching to increases in indicators that represent the overall health of the organization (Kaplan & Norton, 2004).

The indicators your organization ultimately selects to monitor will show progress toward your unique strategic goals. For example, one system might have a high graduation rate, but a low percentage of English Language Learners enrolled in advanced placement courses. Another system might have a high percentage of students with low socioeconomic status who are proficient or better in math, but are not proficient in writing or in the sciences. Both systems can pinpoint indicators to reflect either a growth or decline regarding their stated goals. Either way, they need to show that these desired increases and desired reductions coincide with a deeper and broader implementation of quality leadership coaching.

HERE COMES THE TRICKY PART

In complex systems where multiple initiatives to improve performance are underway at any given time, it is difficult to extract the percentage of success or failure attributable to any single effort. And of course, many factors besides leadership coaching effectiveness contribute to the performance of an organization. However, the link between leadership and student success, and the link between coaching and individual growth, are strong enough to suggest that leadership coaching is a worthy organizational strategy to implement.

Here are a few final ideas to consider as you structure your leadership coaching program evaluation:

- Establish and implement a consistent leadership coaching program in your organization and commit to it for at least three years, which allows you to analyze trend data.
- In order to demonstrate early wins from leadership coaching, use indicators that demonstrate your leadership coaching program is operating as intended. One way to do this is to design an innovation configuration that describes the levels of implementation for each critical component of your leadership coaching initiative. Although

these indicators alone are not adequate to prove leadership coaching is an effective strategy in the long run, they do show returns faster than indicators related to organizational impact, such as leadership promotions, student achievement, and increased graduation rates. They also provide valuable midcourse information about how to adjust and revise coaching and coaching programs.

- Research the records from two to three years *before* the consistent leadership coaching practice begins in order to establish baseline student achievement and organizational performance data.
- When it comes to determining from the baseline points if your leadership coaching initiative is having a positive impact on the system, collect, chart, display, and discuss the same indicators for at least three years.
- Ask the leaders who have been coached to rate their growth as leaders. You can also ask other people in the leader's school building or department to rate the same characteristics through 360 degree evaluations.
- If your system is large enough, compare the growth of schools with participating leaders engaged in leadership coaching to schools without this participation.

Coaching is an organizational strategy for making important and valued changes for people and for the system. As such, it should be evaluated for effectiveness and impact in the same spirit that other important initiatives and strategies in the organization are evaluated. You don't have to go overboard on this; focus on looking at student achievement over time, and at specific information about what coaches did that made a difference for the leaders they coached. This approach to evaluating your leadership coaching strategy provides you with the ability to make good decisions about how to improve your coaching program.

Start a Coaching Movement

chapter 12

The tipping point is that magic moment when an idea, trend, or social behavior crosses a threshold, tips, and spreads like wildfire.

—Malcolm Gladwell (From the jacket cover of *The Tipping Point: How Little Things Can Make a Big Difference,* 2002)

This final chapter will especially resonate with you, if you are reading this book primarily because you are responsible for designing and coordinating the leadership coaching program in your organization. No doubt, you feel responsible for assuring the leadership coaching program in your organization is just as successful in achieving its goals as the elementary school principal is about assuring the reading program produces excellent readers, and the HR director ensuring that the recruiting and hiring process attracts the finest teachers. Just as with any initiative, leaders responsible for leadership coaching programs need to give them a good launch and sustain their implementation; if that is achieved, then they create a movement around leadership coaching as an indispensable and sustainable strategy for leadership success.

REMEMBER WHEN WE "DID" COACHING?

Leadership coaching is a strategy for sustaining the best initiatives of an organization. It is also a powerful innovation in its own right. The last thing program leaders of leadership coaching want to hear is "Remember when we did coaching?" Therefore, with the resolve to treat your leadership coaching initiative with the same care that you do every other district initiative, go back to Chapter 4 and respond to the prompts in the First 100-Day Plan. Your First 100-Day Plan provides focus and momentum whether you are trying to get your leadership coaching strategy off the ground, or revitalizing your existing program.

ORGANIZATIONAL CONSIDERATIONS THAT SUPPORT LEADERSHIP COACHING

When it comes to creating organizational conditions to sustain leadership coaching initiatives, leaders must create ecosystems where leadership coaching can thrive. As with any other initiative, this demands close attention to cultures, organizational alignment, professional development, and quality programs.

Focus Coaching on Critical Initiatives

Programs that are not linked to organizational results become irrelevant and obsolete, especially when budgets are slashed. Leadership coaching programs that lose their focus on essential organizational work eventually lose their value to the organization. Therefore, the number one strategy for sustaining your leadership coaching program is assuring that it is available and offered to change agents—those leaders in the organization doing the best and most difficult work of the organization. These leaders are passionate about their work, but they also ensure that others understand how initiatives align and are coherent with the expressed mission and needs of the organization, and they inspire engagement.

Align the Culture to Coaching

The late Peter Drucker, who is revered as the Father of Management, is thought to have said, "Culture eats strategy for breakfast." What Drucker meant is that even the best strategies fail if the culture is not simultaneously built to support their implementation.

Many leaders say they want a coaching program in their organizations, but not all organizations have cultures aligned with the purpose of coaching. Leaders who find themselves operating in organizations that are not fully prepared to support coaching need to audit their culture for the attitudes, patterns of interaction, policies, and practices that support coaching. Then they need to shore up the organization with cultural structures that support coaching and eliminate or revise existing structures that hinder a healthy culture for coaching.

The cultural conditions that sustain leadership coaching and allow leaders to perform meaningful work are also linked to the sources of on-the-job energy and joy. Since 2009, I have been writing about on-the-job happiness as a source of energy and renewal for leaders who are passionately engaged in meaningful work (Allison & Reeves, 2012; Reeves & Allison, 2009, 2010). In 2011, I began asking leaders to tell me what gives them happiness and energy on the job, and during the work day. In this ongoing study, responses from leaders have rendered hundreds of data points that provide clues about the characteristics of systems that promote energy in people (to participate, please visit www.wisdomout.com and select "participate" and "the happiness research" from the menu).

Sources of Workplace Energy and Joy

What leaders find most energizing on the job has very little to do with taking breaks and escaping the demands of the organization, and more to do with being successful in relationships, problem solving, learning, and making a difference for stakeholders—the very same outcomes transformational leadership coaching seeks to produce. In other words, leaders gain energy from doing the work of the organization. Not surprising, given most educational leaders' penchant for learning, many of these same characteristics also describe job-embedded professional development (Brown-Easton, 2008) and learning organizations (Senge, 1990).

Table 12.1 displays the on-the-job energy sources named by leaders who participated in my study, when they were asked for their top three.

Table 12.1 Sources of On-the-Job Energy and Joy

Sources of Energy and Professional Joy	Percentage of Leaders Who Listed This Source as One of Their Top Three Choices
When I am involved in positive conversations and interactions	27%
When I perceive a benefit to stakeholders	19%
When I get things done on my "to do" list	15%
When I teach, learn, and problem solve	14%
When I accomplish something toward a common goal	13%
When I both give and receive gratitude	5%
When I allow for interludes and stress busters	5%
Other	2%

Source: © Elle Allison, 2012.

If we expect deep and sustained implementation of the most important work of the organization, we cannot leave happiness and energy on the table (Ben-Shahar, 2007). Leadership coaching creates on-the-job energy. It creates interludes of renewal during the workday and stimulates every single one of the energy sources identified by leaders in Table 12.1.

The following inventory (Figure 12.1) reflects the cultural norms that allow leadership coaching to flourish in organizations. What are

Figure 12.1 The Coaching Culture

Strength	Challenge	
_____	_____	1. People in our organization trust each other. "Mistakes" are seen as a given in the creative process.
_____	_____	2. People in our organization know they can explore new ideas and take risks in alignment with the mission of our enterprise.
_____	_____	3. Our organization engages in job-embedded professional development by encouraging and supporting dialogue and peer-to-peer coaching.
_____	_____	4. People in our organization seek to achieve goals that advance our mission and that benefit a greater good.
_____	_____	5. We believe that leaders at all levels grow by taking action and reflecting on the impact of their actions on profit, people, and the planet.
_____	_____	6. People in our organization are not too busy to think together.
_____	_____	7. In our organization, we believe that analysis of early wins and lessons learned leads to innovation, and renewal of people and programs.
_____	_____	8. People in our organization know that they can bring anything up for discussion.
_____	_____	9. In our organization, we value renewal as much as we value the expenditure of energy in pursuit of meaningful work for a greater good.
_____	_____	10. People in our organization believe that most people want to do meaningful work, and create meaningful relationships.

Scoring: If you checked eight to ten of these items as strengths, your organization is primed to support job-embedded practices of coaching. If you checked seven to eight of the items as strengths, your organization has a moderate challenge to create a supportive culture for coaching. If you checked less than seven boxes as strengths, your organization needs to make significant changes in the culture in order to support coaching.

This tool is also available for download at www.WisdomOut.com and www.Corwin.com/Flywheel.

your organization's strengths and challenges? Once you complete the checklist, confirm your assumptions with at least two other colleagues.

Reframe Leadership Coaching

Many educators still believe that leadership coaching is a strategy for intervening with poor performing administrators who are on their way out. Others believe leadership coaching is a good strategy for novice administrators, but not appropriate for veteran leaders who should not require a coach. However, organizations that want to sustain leadership coaching need to reframe it and redefine it from an intervention for poor performers and novice leaders to a development program for high performing leaders—for any agent of change who takes the helm of important work (Gawande, 2011).

Battle Busyness

To be completely honest, one of the biggest culprits that undermine cultures of coaching is "busyness." Ironically, leaders who are not involved in complex and meaningful work often have the greatest sense of busyness. These individuals constantly complain of feeling overwhelmed, either by "fires they need to put out," or tasks and responsibilities they feel they must accomplish that were assigned to them by others (e.g., paperwork, reports, meetings). These leaders are absorbed by activities that Steven Covey (1989) famously refers to as either Quadrant I: Urgent and Important, or Quandrant III: Urgent and Unimportant. Leaders who coach more, lead more. But, if they want to give valuable energy to coaching then these leaders must stop being so darn busy.

Embrace Models of Job-Embedded Professional Development

Leaders need to give more than lip service to implementing all forms of job-embedded professional development, such as coaching. In an issue brief written by leaders in professional development and teacher quality, several formats for job-embedded professional development, including coaching, were identified and recommended (Croft, Coggshall, Dolan, Powers, & Killion, 2010). In organizations where cultures naturally organize to support job-embedded professional development, leadership coaching thrives.

Support Innovation and Experimentation

Action research and open sourcing are two ways to encourage practitioners to take on projects that can create breakthrough results. "Open

Source" refers to a model of innovation that invites people, often from outside roles and disciplines, to invent solutions to problems, or to refine current initiatives in response to changing or emerging needs (Chesbrough, 2006). Both action research and open sourcing welcome practitioners to experiment and improve on the initiatives that funnel down from the central office, and outside researchers to them, which makes leadership coaching particularly relevant and instrumental to the process.

Provide Professional Development in Leadership Coaching

Ensure that more people know how to provide on-the-job coaching to peers, colleagues, and direct reports. Ideally, colleagues offer coaching to each other and ask for coaching from each other as they implement school and district initiatives. Leaders who coach peers and colleagues need to master a simple yet powerful coaching conversation protocol that they can use during the workday. To ensure that more leaders are equipped to coach on the job, how to be a "coaching leader" should be a priority element of your organizational leadership development program. The good news is that most organizations are replete with employees who are eager to add leadership coaching to their repertoire of skills.

A Curriculum for Leadership Coaches

Those who work with designing coaching training programs agree that certain activities are essential to the ongoing support and development of coaches (Bloom, Castagna, Moir, & Warren, 2005; Chen, 2003; Haneberg, 2006). These activities suggest the following learning experiences for leaders and coaches:

- All leaders and all coaches should learn the communication skills used in coaching conversations: listening, asking clarifying and detail questions to reveal assumptions, asking open-ended questions that inspire new thinking, paraphrasing, summarizing, brainstorming, and asking others to commit to action.
- Participate in specific and ongoing learning within quality coach-training programs that include practical experience in coaching with feedback from an experienced coach mentor.
- Coaches should belong to a professional learning community and coaching network in order to refine and learn new coaching skills, methods, and techniques.
- Work with a coach in order to accomplish projects in their own life and work.

- Stay current in the research and best ideas of their specific field, including the standards, current practices, interventions, opportunities, and approaches.
- Acquire specific training in setting up and monitoring projects, and become skilled in using the tools that structure project implementation.

Make Leadership Coaching a Presence in Your Organization: A Smattering of Practical Ideas

I leave you with a number of strategies for making leadership coaching an observable movement in your organization.

- Make it visible: Put up a leadership coaching web page that explains the leadership coaching process, and lists the names of leaders who have completed coach training and are ready and able to coach.
- Hang out a shingle: In the Flywheel program, we give leaders who complete the program signs that say, "I am a leader who coaches" or "I am a coach: Would you like a thought partner?" that they can put on their office or room door (come to www.WisdomOut.com if you'd like to purchase a set of these posters).
- Ask trained coaches to "find someone to coach" at least twice per month.
- Supply a "coaching question of the day" and encourage people to illuminate it for themselves and with colleagues throughout the day (see the Appendix for many examples of good Thought Leadership Questions).
- Include leadership coaching on your data walls, and measure a few basic statistics, such as how many coaching sessions took place that month throughout the organization.
- Make leadership coaching a service provided to central office and site-based leaders as part of their administrative contracts.
- Develop cadres of coaches, either internal or external to the organization, who understand the context of the leader's work and provide job-embedded coaching that relates to the real-life work of coachees.
- Link the leadership coaching program to leadership skills and professional standards as a simultaneous by-product of leading projects that create needed change.
- Judge the effectiveness of your leadership coaching program on the forward motion of important organizational initiatives.
- Make leadership coaching available to leaders at all levels (teacher leaders, administrators, project leaders) who are at the helm of

crucial strategies and innovative projects to advance the goals of the organization.

- Provide professional development in leadership coaching skills for all leaders who want to coach their colleagues, peers, and direct reports.
- Hold leadership innovation fairs where leaders who worked through a coaching project can display and explain their successes.
- Invite coaches and leaders who have been coached to participate in a panel discussion on the benefits of coaching. Videotape the discussion and put it on the district leadership coaching web page.
- Support your leadership coaches with a coach mentor who can provide advice, ideas, and share their experiences.
- Ensure that leadership coaches focus on asking powerful questions that promote thinking, learning, and commitment to action in lieu of giving answers and advice.

FINAL WORDS

As a student and practitioner in organizational learning, my passion is to design processes that develop people, teams, and organizations so that they can create a better self, a better organization, and a better world. My greatest joy is to teach leaders to coach their peers, colleagues, and team members as they go about doing the best work of the organization. This book is offered to you in that spirit—to encourage you to embrace leadership coaching as a powerful approach to support and develop the people around you.

Appendix: Thought Leadership Questions

To Promote Self-Renewal

- How are you currently taking care of yourself?
- What do you need now to perform at your best?
- What do you want to learn next?
- What will renewal allow you to accomplish?
- Who can you vent with? Who can you debrief with? Who can you think with?

To Increase and Focus Energy

- What can you let go of now?
- What do you need to reenergize now?
- What do you need to say no to?
- How will you respond to new requests?

To Play a Bigger Game and Strive for a Greater Good

- What is your purpose in this project, in your family, in life?
- What do you need to learn in order to create a more compelling future?
- How can this project impact the future, and a wide circle of stakeholders and shareholders?
- What legacy do you want to leave through this project or work?

To Encourage Action in the Face of Loss

- What is the new reality?
- What are people and customers asking for?

- What are the needs of each stakeholder group?
- What can be done immediately to support the people affected?
- What action will show others that this situation will not get you down?
- What is the next milestone you are working toward? What will people, stakeholders, and customers need in the next year?

To Express a Compelling Vision

- What is your new vision?
- What about the new reality contributes to the vision?
- How does your new vision help others to resist the "pull of the past"?
- What is the bigger picture here?
- What will you celebrate?

To Learn From Loss and Resilience

- What is the silver lining in this situation?
- How does this loss make it easier for you to move forward?
- What is the best opportunity resulting from this situation?
- What has this loss or challenge clarified for you?
- What are the takeaway lessons here?
- What do you want to learn next?

To Lead People Through an Implementation Dip, or a Sense of Powerlessness

- Where have you seen the strongest momentum up to this point?
- What is still missing? What is needed?
- What are you not getting to?
- How can you use your talents to improve this situation?
- What requests could you make to move this forward?
- What do you feel like doing? If you could do one thing now, what would it be?
- What do you notice about yourself when you take action?
- What do you need to get scheduled?
- What do you need to ask someone else to do for you? What do you need to communicate?
- What do you need to stop in order to make room for something else?
- What do you need to get started on?
- Where do you feel you have leverage?

To Influence Others

- What did your presence in this meeting (or other event) add in a positive sense?
- How can you be helpful here without taking over for others?
- What works for you when you are effective in increasing optimism in others?
- Who needs your compassionate perspective?
- What could you do or say in this situation that would empower the people around you?

To Create Relationships and Build Teams

- Who is on your go-to team? Are they the right people for this project? Who else needs to be on that team?
- Who can open doors for you? How will you approach them?
- How will you initiate communication (with a person, group)?
- What conversations do you want to start? With whom?
- Who needs you to notice how great they are in this situation?
- Who has influence in this matter? What would their support mean to you?
- What ten relationships do you want to start paying attention to?

To Sustain Relationships

- How do you usually take care of important relationships?
- Is this a relationship that matters to the success of your accomplishment?
- What is great about the quality of your conversations with this person or team?
- What is missing from the quality of your conversations with this person or team?
- Are " indiscussables" creeping into this relationship?

To Increase Communication for Relationships

- What is the worst that could happen if you confided in someone about this? Who could that be?
- What are you pretending to want versus what you really want?
- How have you ensured that people know what you wish to accomplish?
- What do you really want to do or say now? What is stopping you?
- What difficult conversation have you been avoiding?

To Become More Aware of Your Impact on Relationships

- Who would appreciate your attention? What would that allow the person to do?
- Who admires you or loves you? What does that tell you about yourself?
- Who do you interact with from day to day whom you haven't asked to contribute?
- Who looks like an "outsider" to this project, but has an important perspective?
- Who do you appreciate? For what, specifically? What do you need to say to this person or group?
- Is there anyone you are taking for granted?
- What stereotypes or assumptions are you using?

To Respond to the Pressure of a Difficult Relationship

- What are you settling for in this relationship?
- What is at the root of your mistrust? Is it something you know about or heard?
- What do you get from this relationship?
- Can you ask more of this relationship?
- Do you want more from this relationship?
- Does this relationship give you energy to do the most important work you do?
- What conversation do you need to have with this person or team?
- What are you tempted to control in this relationship?
- Are you open to this person or team? Are you easy to talk to?
- What are you taking personally?
- What are the indiscussables? What scares you about this?
- How can you vent your emotions before talking with this person or group?

To Give and Receive, Teach, and Learn

- Who needs your wisdom?
- Who can support you?
- What would you ask for if you could? What will you offer?
- What are you learning? What are you teaching others?
- Which of the goals in your organization have to do with developing people?
- Who are you coaching or mentoring?

To Inspire Gratitude

- Whom are you grateful for?
- Whom do you need to thank?
- How will you thank them?
- Who has helped you achieve significant goals?

To Inspire Great Meetings

- What are your goals for this meeting, event, or conversation?
- What data do you need to gather before this event?
- Are there underlying goals that are as important as the obvious goals?
- What important decisions will you need to make related to this issue?
- What do you see yourself doing to produce the desired outcomes?

To Help Someone Reflect on a Meeting

- As you reflect back on the meeting, conversation, or event, how do you think it went?
- What did you see people doing or saying that made you feel that way?
- What do you recall about your own behavior and feelings during this event?
- How did the outcome compare with what you had planned?
- What would you do the same in the future? What would you change?

To Give and Receive Feedback

- Who needs you to give them feedback? How available and willing are you to support them?
- What is your accountability in this effort? Is there someone you can debrief with about that?
- What feedback will you ask for that might shift your perspective?
- Where do you or others need a new level of performance?
- Who will pay a price if you don't give feedback?
- When are you or others more or less open to feedback?

To Focus Energy Where It Can Make the Biggest Difference

- What is the worst case scenario if you pay cursory attention to the people who are resistant? What would result?
- When is it appropriate to use the system's established procedures to influence individuals who want to kill a change initiative?

- Where is your energy going in this project?
- What is causing this project to slow down?

To Consider Different Perspectives and Realities

- What are you missing here?
- What data are you finding helpful?
- Are there other key information sources?
- What do you need to learn?
- What are you "sure of"? Is it preventing you from seeing another point of view?
- Who agrees with you? Who disagrees with you?
- What is the opposite point of view?

To Look at Evidence and to Make Decisions

- Is it time for a decision?
- What is the decision that is needed?
- What problem will this decision solve?
- Who will benefit or not from this decision?
- Does everyone agree on the problem and the decision?
- When you said _____, did you mean _____?
- How are you? What do you feel about this challenge or opportunity?

To Examine Patterns

- What is your role in this decision?
- What are you known for in the groups you belong to?
- What are the risks to responding in your usual way?
- What are the benefits to responding in your usual way?
- What emotions do you have about this matter?
- What emotions cause you to have a more positive effect?

References

Allison, E. (2008, Winter). Coaching teachers for school transformation. *Principal Matters, 75,* 9–10.

Allison, E., & Reeves, D. B. (2012). *Renewal coaching fieldbook.* San Francisco, CA: Jossey-Bass.

Amabile, T. M., & Kramer, S. J. (2011). *The progress principal: Using small wins to ignite joy, engagement, and creativity at work.* Cambridge, MA: Harvard Business Review Press.

Apatow, R. (1998). *The spiritual art of dialogue: Mastering communication for personal growth, relationships, and the workplace.* Rochester, VT: Inner Traditions.

Argyris, C. (1993). *Knowledge for action.* San Francisco, CA: Jossey-Bass.

Ashkenas, R. (2010). *Simply effective: How to cut through complexity in your organization and get things done.* Boston, MA: Harvard Business Press.

Axtell, P. (2009). *How to be a great coach.* Moline, IL: Contextual Program Designs.

Ben-Shahar, T. (2007). *Happier.* New York: McGraw-Hill.

Bloom, G., Castagna, C., Moir, E., & Warren, B. (2005). *Blended coaching: Skills and strategies to support principal development.* Thousand Oaks, CA: Corwin.

Bossidy, L., & Charan, R. (2002). *Execution: The discipline of getting things done.* New York: Crown Business.

Boyatzis, R., & McKee, A. (2005). *Resonant leadership.* Boston, MA: Harvard Business School Press.

Braun, L. (2009). *In case of emergency, ask question.* United States: Thought Partners.

Brown-Easton, L. (2008). Powerful designs for professional learning (2nd ed.). Oxford, OH: National Staff Development Council.

Chen, C. (2003). *Coaching training.* Alexandria, VA: ASTD Press.

Chesbrough, H. W. (2006). *Open business models: How to thrive in the new innovation landscape.* Cambridge, MA: Harvard Business School Press.

Chodron, P. (1994). *Start where you are: A guide to compassionate living.* Boston, MA: Shambhala Publications.

Costa, A., & Garmston, R. (1994). *Cognitive coaching: A foundation for renaissance schools.* Norwood, MA: Christopher-Gordon.

Covey, S. (1989). *The 7 habits of highly successful people.* New York: Fireside.

Croft, A., Coggshall, J. G., Dolan, M., Powers, E., & Killion, J. (2010). *Job embedded professional development: What it is, who is responsible, and how to get it done well* (Issue brief). Washington, DC: The National Comprehensive Center for Teacher Quality, Mid-Atlantic Comprehensive Center, and the National Staff Development Council.

Cummings, T. G., & Worley, C. G. (2005). *Organization development and change.* Cincinnati, OH: Cengage Learning.

Daly, P. H., & Watkins, M. (2006). *The first 90 days in government: Critical success strategies for new public managers at all levels.* Boston, MA: Harvard Business School Press.

de Bono, E. (1992). *Serious creativity: Using the power of lateral thinking to create new ideas.* New York: HarperCollins.

Denning, P. J., & Dunham, R. (2010). *The innovator's way: Essential practices for successful innovation.* Cambridge: Massachusetts Institute of Technology.

Dieken, C. (2009). *Talk less, say more: 3 habits to influence others and make things happen.* Hoboken, NJ: Wiley.

Eddington, A. S. (1928). *The nature of the physical world.* New York: Macmillan.

Fink, D., & Hargreaves, A. (2006). *Sustainable leadership.* San Francisco, CA: Jossey-Bass.

Frost, P. J. (2002). *Toxic emotions at work: How compassionate managers handle pain and conflict.* Boston, MA: Harvard Business School Press.

Fullan, M. (1991). *The new meaning of educational change* (2nd ed.). New York: Teachers College Press.

Fullan, M. (1993). *Change force: Probing the depths of education reform.* London, UK: Falmer Press.

Fullan, M. (2001a). *Leading in a culture of change.* San Francisco, CA: Jossey-Bass.

Fullan, M. (2001b). *The new meaning of educational change* (3rd ed.). New York: Teachers College Press.

Fullan, M. (2002). The change leader. *Educational Leadership, 59*(8), 16–21.

Fullan, M. (2005). *The new meaning of educational change: A quarter of a century of learning.* New York: Teachers College Press.

Gawande, A. (2011, October 3). Personal best. *The New Yorker Online Magazine.*

Gladwell, M. (2002). *The tipping point: How little things can make a big difference.* New York: Little, Brown.

Goldsmith, M., & Reiter, M. (2007). *What got you here won't get you there: How successful people become even more successful.* New York: Hyperion.

Goulston, M. (2010). *Just listen.* New York: AMACON.

Hamel, G. (2009, February). Moonshots for management. *Harvard Business Review.*

Haneberg, L. (2006). *Coaching basics.* Alexandria, VA: ASTD Press.

Hargrove, R. A. (2007). *The masterful coaching fieldbook: Grow your business, multiply your profits, win the talent war!* San Francisco, CA: Wiley.

Hattie, J. (2009). *Visible learning: A synthesis of over 800 meta-analyses relating to achievement.* London, UK: Routledge.

Hess, F. M. (2010). *Education unbound: The promise and practice of greenfield schooling.* Alexandria, VA: ASCD Press.

International Coach Federation. (2008). *ICF Professional Coaching Core Competencies.* Lexington, KY: Author. Retrieved from http://www.coachfederation.org/includes/media/docs/CoreCompEnglish.pdf

Isaacs, W. (1999). *Dialogue and the art of thinking together: A pioneering approach to communicating in business and life.* New York: Doubleday.

Johnson, S. (2010). *Where good ideas come from: The natural history of innovation.* New York: Riverhead.

Joyce, B., & Showers, B. (1995). *Student achievement through staff development.* White Plains, NY: Longman.

Kahane, A. (2004). *Solving tough problems: An open way of talking, listening, and creating new realities.* San Francisco, CA: Berrett-Kohler.

Kaplan, R. S., & Norton, D. P. (2004). *Strategy maps: Converting intangible assets into tangible outcomes.* Boston, MA: Harvard Business School Press.

Kilburg, R. (2006). *Executive wisdom: Coaching and the emergence of virtuous leaders.* Washington, DC: American Psychological Association.

Klimek, K. J., Ritzenhein, E., & Sullivan, K. D. (2008). *Generative leadership: Shaping new futures for today's schools.* Thousand Oaks, CA: Corwin.

Koltko-Rivera, M. E. (2006). Rediscovering the later version of Maslow's hierarchy of needs: Self-transcendence and opportunities for theory, research, and unification. *Review of General Psychology, 10*(4), 302–317.

Kotter, J. P. (2007, January). Leading change: Why transformation efforts fail. *Harvard Business Review, 85*(1), 96–103.

Kouzes, J. M., & Pozner, B. Z. (2003). *The leadership challenge.* San Francisco, CA: Jossey-Bass.

Landsberg, M. (2003). *The tao of coaching.* London, UK: Profile Books.

Leithwood, K., Seashore Louis, K., Anderson, S., & Wahlstom, K. (2004). *How leadership influences student learning.* New York: Wallace Foundation.

Marquardt, M. (2005). *Leading with questions: How leaders find the right solutions by knowing what to ask.* San Francisco, CA: Jossey-Bass.

Merriam, S. B., & Caffarella, R. S. (1999). *Learning in adulthood: A comprehensive guide* (2nd ed.). San Francisco, CA: Jossey-Bass.

Mezirow, J. (2000). Learning to think like an adult: Core concepts of transformation theory. In J. Mezirow & Associates (Eds.), *Learning as transformation: Critical perspectives on a theory in progress* (pp. 3–34). San Francisco, CA: Jossey-Bass.

Moss-Kanter, R. (2010, September). How to do well *and* do good. *MIT Sloan Management Review,* Fall Journal.

Mycoskie, B. (2011). *Start something that matters.* New York: Spiegel & Grau.

Nichols, M. (1995). *The lost art of listening: How learning to listen can improve relationships.* New York: The Guilford Press.

O'Neill, M. B. (2000). *Executive coaching with backbone and heart: A systems approach to engaging leaders with their challenges.* San Francisco, CA: Jossey-Bass.

O'Reilly, C., & Tushman, M. L. (1997). *Winning through innovation: A practical guide to leading organizational change and renewal.* Boston, MA: Harvard Business School Press.

Peters, T. (2001, March). Rule #3: Leadership is confusing as hell. *Fast Company Magazine.* Retrieved from http://www.fastcompany.com/42575/rule-3-leadership-confusing-hell

Pink, D. (2009). *Drive: The surprising truth about what motivates us.* New York: Riverhead Books.

Reeves, D. B., & Allison, E. (2009). *Renewal coaching: Sustainable change for individuals and organizations.* San Francisco, CA: Jossey-Bass.

Reeves, D. B., & Allison, E. (2010). *Renewal coaching workbook.* San Francisco, CA: Jossey-Bass.

Sanders, L. (2009). *Every patient tells a story: Medical mysteries and the art of diagnosis.* New York: Random House.

Schmoker, M. (2011). *Focus: Evaluating the essentials to radically improve student achievement.* Alexandria, VA: ASCD Press.

Senge, P. M. (1990). *The fifth discipline: The art and practice of the learning organization.* New York: Doubleday.

Senge, P. M., Ross, R., Smith, B., Roberts, C., & Kleiner, A. (1994). *The fifth discipline fieldbook: Strategies and tools for building a learning organization.* New York: Doubleday.

Senge, P. M., Scharmer, C. O., Jaworski, J., & Flowers, B. S. (2005). *Presence: An exploration of profound change in people, organizations, and society.* New York: Currency/Doubleday.

Shoshanna, B. (2003). *Zen and the art of falling in love.* New York: Simon & Schuster.

Sims, C., & Johnson, H. L. (2012). *Scrum: A breathtakingly brief and agile preface.* San Mateo, CA: Dymaxicon.

Sternberg, R. J. (2000). Intelligence and wisdom. In R. J. Sternberg (Ed.), *Handbook of intelligence* (pp. 631–650). Cambridge, UK: Cambridge University Press.

Sternberg, R. J. (2003). *Wisdom, intelligence, and creativity synthesized.* Cambridge, UK: Cambridge University Press.

Stoltzfus, T. (2008). *Coaching questions: A coach's guide to powerful asking skills.* Virginia Beach, VA: Author.

Storber, D. R., & Grant, A. M. (Eds.). (2006). *Evidenced-based coaching handbook: Putting best practices to work for your coachee.* Hoboken, NJ: Wiley.

Vanderburg, M., & Stephens, D. (2010). The impact of literacy coaches. *The Elementary School Journal, 3*(1), 141–163.

Weisbord, M. R. (1987). *Productive workplaces: Organizing and managing for dignity, meaning, and community.* San Francisco, CA: Jossey-Bass.

Wittrock, M. C. (1992). Generative learning processes of the brain. *Educational Psychologist, 27*(4), 531–541.

Index